The ScrumMaster Study Guide

The ScrumMaster Study Guide
James Schiel
978-1-4398-5991-9

Enterprise-Scale Agile Software Development
James Schiel
978-1-4398-0321-9

Requirements Engineering for Software and Systems
Phillip A. Laplante
978-1-4200-6467-4

Building Software: A Practioner's Guide
Nikhilesh Krishnamurthy and Amitabh Saran
978-0-8493-7303-9

Global Software Development Handbook
Raghvinder Sangwan, Matthew Bass, Neel Mullick, Daniel J. Paulish,
and Juergen Kazmeier
978-0-8493-9384-6

Antipatterns: Identification, Refactoring, and Management
Phillip A. Laplante and Colin J. Neill
978-0-8493-2994-4

Software Engineering Quality Practices
Ronald Kirk Kandt
978-0-8493-4633-0

The ScrumMaster Study Guide

James Schiel

CRC Press
Taylor & Francis Group
Boca Raton   London   New York

CRC Press is an imprint of the
Taylor & Francis Group, an **informa** business
AN AUERBACH BOOK

CRC Press
Taylor & Francis Group
6000 Broken Sound Parkway NW, Suite 300
Boca Raton, FL 33487-2742

© 2012 by Taylor & Francis Group, LLC
CRC Press is an imprint of Taylor & Francis Group, an Informa business

No claim to original U.S. Government works

Printed in the United States of America on acid-free paper
Version Date: 20111003

International Standard Book Number: 978-1-4398-5991-9 (Hardback)

Library of Congress Cataloging-in-Publication Data

Schiel, James.
    The ScrumMaster Study Guide / James Schiel.
        p. cm. -- (Applied software engineering series)
    Includes bibliographical references and index.
    ISBN 978-1-4398-5991-9 (alk. paper)
    1. Agile software development. 2. Scrum (Computer software development) I. Title.

QA76.76.D47S2956 2012
005.1--dc23   2011027001

Visit the Taylor & Francis Web site at
http://www.taylorandfrancis.com

and the CRC Press Web site at
http://www.crcpress.com

Contents

SECTION II Questions Frequently
Asked in CSM Training

Preface

Following the completion of my first book (*Enterprise-Scale Agile Software Development*, CRC Press, Boca Raton, FL, 2010), I found myself wishing I could put more information into it. There was more I wanted to say about agile development and Scrum, but I was limited by time and my publisher's desire to publish a book that was actually close to the size I told him it would be, so I put the wraps on that book in January 2009 and, after a bit of a break from writing, proposed a new book. I got the working idea for the second book simply by teaching CSM (Certified ScrumMaster) and CSPO (Certified Scrum Product Owner) classes. I get a lot of questions in those classes, and I often get a lot of the same questions across many classes (I have taught over 100 CSM/CSPO classes and an uncounted number of seminars and workshops). In many cases, I have asked my students to write their questions down on Post-its®, and I would answer them at the end of the class for all those who wanted to stay and listen. Rather than throw all those questions away (which, unfortunately, I did at first), they represented to me areas of interest for my students and, as a resource, were priceless. As a result, I found myself with a significant stack of Post-its as fodder for this book.

This book, then, is a "reanswering" of many of the questions that I have been asked during and after CSM and CSPO classes. I do not expect that my answers are the best answers or that my answers are the only answers. My intention is not to define Scrum or agile or to say that I have all the answers. As with my first book, my expectation is that you read, learn, and try what makes sense. If the answer I provide does not work for you but a similar version of an answer that you create from my suggestion works— perfect! That is all I am trying to do.

My hope is that you enjoy reading this book, that the writing speaks to you, and that you find the content useful and beneficial. I hope also, if you are reading and saying, "Hey, I've always wanted to author a book," that the fact that you are reading my second effort will inspire you to grasp the opportunity and do the same. The more information we, collectively, accumulate, the faster we can accomplish what the Scrum Alliance has set out to do, to "[transform] the world of work."

Acknowledgments

Here I sit, once again, putting the finishing touches on the draft manuscript of a book. I am 38,000 feet in the air, flying home to Philadelphia from Europe. This trip has been particularly satisfying because the customer I was visiting has begun the final polishing of a product prior to release, and the mood of the organization is a complete turnaround from that associated with the previous version. Unlike the first version, which was built in a waterfall project, this new version was built from day one in an agile project with 20+ Scrum teams. These new Scrum teams accomplished an incredible amount of work in a short period of time. The product itself was demonstrable on any given day—my customer even began running monthly demonstrations of the working product for people in the company who wanted to see it. The number of defects is considerably less than the number of known defects at the same time in the previous project. The project lead (who coordinates across the Scrum teams and the rest of the organization) is happy, and the Product Owners have smiles on their faces. The product is much better than it was before, and they know it.

If my family and I could survive on well wishes and good feelings, I would be set for life.

In this, my second book, I want to acknowledge the people who made this book possible by either being the source of my experiences or being in the trenches with me, dealing with the problems and making it all make sense in the end. I'll try to be brief.

First, of course, I must thank my family for their patience and their love; for being there when I come home and for not being too choked up when I leave; for putting up with daily e-mails, text messages, and iChat and Skype sessions; for saying "Scrum" and "Sprint" without laughing; and for being the core and the reason for everything I do. Thank you, Donna (the love of my life) and my children Rebecca, Melanie, Jacob, and Rachel. My thanks also to Cheryl Brokaw for being there when work called both my wife and me away at the same time—for being calm and reliable in some of the weirdest situations. Thank you to Leah Halpern and Ron Bershad (the "in-laws") and Phyllis Schiel (my mother) for being such caring grandparents to my children, who value your visits. You help me keep them honest and in touch with reality. To my father, Frank, who passed away in 1996, the example you set for me years ago still keeps me focused on being pragmatic in my work. Thank you.

My thanks also to John Wyzalek, my publisher, who I believe at this point looks at my predictions for finishing manuscripts with the same assurance that many of us look at waterfall project schedules that spell out the tasks for the next several months. Notice, John, that this manuscript was not as delayed as the last one. I'm getting better!

To Dr. Phil LaPlante, the editor of the series to which this book and my previous book are a part, thank you for giving me a chance. I hope I have managed to add to your series the type of information and approach you wanted.

To my customers and friends around the world who keep me busy and keep depending on me to provide high-quality training and good customer experiences, thank you for continuing to believe in me.

Thank you to my friends and customers in Europe and the United States (you know who you are) who have been so much fun to work with, teach, and learn from.

Finally, of course, to all of the team members (including ScrumMasters and Product Owners) on all of the Scrum teams I have worked with who are responsible for turning coaching into actual practice: Your courage to do something different, give it your best, and make it happen despite the challenges and obstacles is a real testimony to what people can do when they decide to work together to make things happen. Scrum says that you, the developers and team members, are the ones who are truly committed. The rest of us are involved. Well, it was all of you that showed what true commitment can accomplish. This book is dedicated to all of you.

About the Author

Jim Schiel has over 28 years of experience in software development, research-and-development (R&D) management, agile development, and Scrum in highly regulated industries. He has been a Certified ScrumMaster (CSM) since 2005 and a Certified Scrum Professional (CSP) and Certified Scrum Trainer (CST) since 2006.

Jim's career started in 1985 when he began working for Siemens Medical Solutions. He managed various development teams, ranging in size from 5 to 80 developers; he instituted iterative project management processes. At Siemens, Jim transitioned an organization of 1,200 developers from waterfall and various iterative models to agile development using Scrum and Extreme Programming (XP) concepts. Jim left Siemens in 2008 to begin working as an agile coach and trainer and in 2009 founded Artisan Software Consulting. Artisan provides coaching, training, and consulting to organizations attempting large-scale transitions to agile development using lean software development principles, Scrum, XP, and kanban approaches.

Jim has been training for over 7 years and has trained more than 1,100 students. He currently teaches Certified ScrumMaster courses and Certified Scrum Product Owner courses and provides workshops on advanced Scrum techniques, user stories, agile in management, and more. Jim's book, *Enterprise-Scale Agile Software Development*, published in 2010 by CRC Press, covers much of his experiences managing and guiding large-scale transformations.

Jim lives in Lafayette Hill, Pennsylvania, with his wife, Donna, and children Rebecca, Melanie, Jacob, and Rachel.

1

Introduction

So, you have either recently attended a Certified ScrumMaster (CSM) training, you are going to attend a CSM training, or you are thinking about attending CSM training. Good for you! That is an excellent first step toward leveraging Scrum and making your organization truly agile. However, there is one lesson I would like to make sure you understand, no matter who you are, before you look at Scrum as the beginning and the end of your agile transformation.

Scrum is *not* enough.

Yes, that is right. Scrum is not enough. By itself, Scrum can do some wonderful things. I have seen good teams become really good. I have seen performance, quality, and productivity all increase just because of Scrum. However, I have also seen that there is a ceiling regarding how good you can get with just Scrum. There is a limit to how much better you can be. If you want more than what Scrum can provide, you have to supplement it with good solid engineering practices, a solid engineering infrastructure, some cultural and behavioral practices from Extreme Programming (XP), and a lot of organizational self-discipline. For more information, see "Does Scrum Work by Itself?" in Chapter 13.

This book is intended for all those newly minted ScrumMasters, Product Owners, or students about to attend a CSM or CSPO (Certified Scrum Product Owner) class, and for those developers and managers who are simply curious, to give you a detailed description of agile and Scrum from the eyes of the people who asked the questions while they were learning about Scrum. If you are a manager thinking about starting an agile transition or an employee engaged in an agile transition, read my first book first and then come back to this book once you are ready to create Scrum teams—the information in this book will help you make many of the practical, operational decisions you will need to make as your new

Scrum teams start getting busy. The book is all about answering many of the common questions I have been asked over the years. Since many of these questions are asked repeatedly, I decided to fill a book with them in the hopes that this book might sit alongside other books that teach Scrum and agile development but do not address some of the details and unusual situations that you might face in the real world.

One thing I discovered during the journey of writing this book was that a lot of questions were specifically about using Scrum. Not what it was, but how to do it. For example, we teach about Sprint Planning in the CSM class, but not many trainers are able to spend the time beyond the basics of why we do it, who is in attendance at the meeting, what we do during the meeting, and what should be the outcome of the meeting. Some trainers do simulations during our classes, but this does not really provide much more than a fundamental understanding of Scrum. So, I decided to combine all of the questions together into the first major section of the book, what I call "The Practical Guide to Scrum." This section has its own introduction, so I will save what I have to say for then. Let it suffice for now that this section of the book tries to provide a way (not the only way) for you to walk out of your CSM training and put Scrum to use right away. I hope you will find it useful.

The remaining chapters in the second part of the book are built around questions that are commonly asked during my CSM classes but do not really fit into the first section. These chapters are built around their own themes:

- **"About Agile Development."** Agile development is more than a development process. It is a concept, and it will frequently challenge what you thought was right in software development. Chapter 11 is dedicated to questions about agile.
- **"About Scrum."** Scrum is a unique framework. It does not actually talk about developing software and, in fact, has been used in many instances that have nothing to do with writing software. Typically, it challenges many of the ways we work as developers and managers and requires a level of self-discipline that many organizations have to work to achieve once they have adopted Scrum as their agile framework. Chapter 12 is dedicated to questions about Scrum.
- **"Using Scrum."** Once you have started using Scrum, you will begin to experience some benefits and some new situations. Chapter 13 is dedicated to answering questions about Scrum and Scrum teams once they are up and running.

- **"Agile Product Management."** Many of the questions I am asked have to do with getting the product out the door. Scrum and the CSM class specifically tend to worry about the "definition" phase of software development, without addressing concerns about release planning, setting customer expectations, and simply starting from scratch with a whole new product. Chapter 14 is dedicated to questions about managing products in an agile environment.
- **"Agile Development Dysfunctions."** Unfortunately, unusual stuff can happen when using agile development. Sometimes, it is obvious when something is going wrong; sometimes it is not, even though you might feel that something is not quite right. Chapter 15 is dedicated to questions about unusual activity and dysfunctions seen when using agile development methods.

I hope this book illuminates some aspects of agile development and Scrum that might have previously been difficult to comprehend. My answers may not always be the best ones for you, but I can promise that my answers will at least provide a starting point, a talking point from which to find the answers you need in your organization.

Section I

The Practical Guide to Scrum

I am told by those who did me the great favor of buying and reading my first book that one of its greatest strengths is the practical presentation of the content. I am glad to hear this as I am a very practical person by nature. There are some things I definitely get carried away with, but the practice of software development and project management are not on that list. For me, I know that agile is working for my customers when their customers are happier with the latest version of software than they were before. If that is accomplished by doing some agile practices, but not all, or by doing Scrum, but differently than written—that is okay by me. I might suggest figuring out how to fit in those missing practices or try to use more and more of Scrum as defined, but that is up to my customers to decide if they want to do it; it is not up to me whether they use "pure" agile.

My most important goal for this book was to ensure that it included some practical advice on how to use Scrum and agile development. Please note, I am not suggesting that this is the only way to use Scrum and agile, or that Scrum and other agile practices are supposed to be used as suggested in this section. Use Scrum and agile as you see fit. But please, if you can, at least start with what I am suggesting and then go from there.

2

An Agile Product Development Life Cycle

Scrum and, for the most part, agile development are based on empirical process control. That means that feedback loops are used to inspect what is going on in product development and to provide an opportunity to update the plan to deal with changes in vision, goal, cost, or requirement. When you examine the entire product life cycle of a product built with agile development, you can see the same concepts of inspection and adaptation going on at all levels.

As you can see in Figure 2.1, a simple agile product development life cycle can be defined as consisting primarily of "backlog development" (during which the Product Backlog is built, maintained, and groomed for development purposes) and "software development" (during which actual software is built). In the software development track, you can see the various "inspect-and-adapt" loops that are typical in the agile project:

- **Release Planning/Release Sprint.** In Release Planning, the content of the release is planned. In the Release Sprint, the content of the release is reviewed and decisions made regarding what needs to go into the next release. A final review of the product can take place at the end of the Release Sprint to help set the stage for the development goals of the next release.
- **Development Sprints (Sprint Planning and Sprint Review).** During Sprint Planning, the goals of the Sprint are determined. In Sprint Review, the goals of the Sprint are reviewed to see which were satisfied and which were not, setting the stage for the planning in the next Sprint.

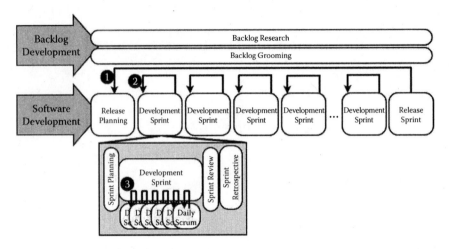

FIGURE 2.1
The agile product development cycle and its built-in inspect-and-adapt feedback loops. (Loop 1 is the release loop; loop 2 is the Sprint loop; and loop 3 is the daily loop. Each of these loops represents a point in time at which work is reviewed and next steps are decided.)

- **Development Sprints (Daily Scrum Meetings).** During the Sprint, Daily Scrum meetings are used to determine how well the team is performing against its goals and decisions are made with regard to how the next several hours of work will be done.

3

Release Planning and "Iteration Zero"

INTRODUCTION

Prior to the beginning of a project, it is a good idea to spend some time getting ready for the project. If possible, of course, you will want to do a lot of what I discuss in this section during the latter half of a previous project (if there is a previous project). Regardless of whether you do it all in one or two workshops or whether you do it as an "iteration zero"—do it.

Here are the things you will want to think about as preparatory steps for planning a new release (Figure 3.1):

- Product Backlog preparation (prioritization and selection of items for the project or release, including sizing of the items by the Scrum teams)
- Setting the Sprint schedule
- Staffing of Scrum teams
- Training of Scrum teams
- Review/revise DONEness definitions
- Creation of or modification to an architecture definition
- Grooming for first Sprint

In the remainder of this chapter, I review the items listed in detail, describing not necessarily how you should hold the various meetings and workshops required to create the information, but rather what these items should be able to address by the time you are finished.

Before we continue talking about Release Planning, we should discuss the concept of story points and velocity. Both are integral to Release Planning and are referenced frequently in this chapter. These terms are defined as follows:

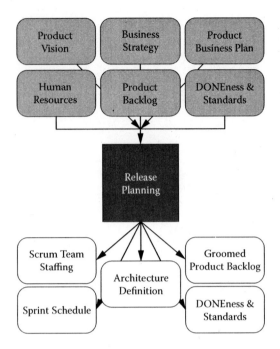

FIGURE 3.1
Inputs and outputs of the Release Planning meeting.

- **Story Point**—a unitless, relative unit of measure that agile teams (generally Scrum and XP [Extreme Programming] teams) use to indicate their estimation of the complexity of a backlog item, or "user story." User stories that are relatively simple will be assigned low story point values. Stories that are complex will be assigned higher story point values. Stories of a similar complexity will have a similar story point value. When teams become experienced in this method of effort estimation, they are much more able to commit consistently to what they can complete in each Sprint, and their predictability as they complete the backlog items on the Release Backlog becomes increasingly better over time.
- **Velocity.** Specifically, velocity is the moving average of the sum of the story point sizes of the backlog items *completed* each Sprint during the previous three or four Sprints. Velocity tells you how much work the team is completing each Sprint so that you can predict where they will be in two Sprints, three Sprints, and so on. At the same time, velocity is absolute in terms of user story DONEness; either a story is done or it is not. There is no partial credit for work almost completed.

A five-story-point story is worth 0 points to a team's velocity if not completed or 5 points if completed. There is no middle ground. This is the primary reason why velocity is usually calculated as a moving average over the last three or four Sprints—the averaging tends to "soften" the spikes caused by nearly complete Stories.

PRODUCT BACKLOG PREPARATION

Getting your Product Backlog ready for the next release of your product (often called a "Release Backlog," terminology I use in this chapter and throughout the book) can be among the most difficult aspects of your release planning. For a Release Backlog to be ready for the project to begin, it must meet several criteria:

Prioritized: For Scrum to work, it requires that the work that the Scrum teams need to do be ordered in one manner or another. I avoid, for the purposes of this book, discussing the various mechanisms and criteria for ordering; they are many, varied, and subjective. Prioritization can include factors of risk (discussed in the next paragraph), information discovery value, ability to create profit, applicability to the strategic plan, market value depreciation, and so on. Without an ordered Release Backlog, there is no reasonable way to ensure that what the Scrum teams will build is sufficiently valuable.

When ordering your backlog, consider how you want to handle risk. Do you want the riskiest backlog items done early in case there is a problem? Perhaps you want to get some easy stuff done first, move on to some risky stuff, and then load the rest of the project with more straightforward items that will allow the teams a lesser challenge during the late Sprints in the project.

Sized: To decide how much will fit into a release, it is necessary to have every potential item on the Product Backlog sized by the Scrum teams. During these workshops, your Scrum teams will also put size estimates on Product Backlog items that do not yet have a size estimate; combined, this is usually how you get a sized Product Backlog. If you do not yet have Scrum teams, you will have to use a more traditional method to create the initial sizing of the backlog. I discussed one method, called "T-shirt sizing," in *Enterprise-Scale Agile Software Development* (Schiel 2010, 199).

Scoped: A Release Backlog is intended to reflect the amount of work that can be completed in a given timeframe and with a predetermined amount of human and other resources. The difficult part, of course, is trying to determine how much of a backlog is too much. Whether you use T-shirt sizes, story points, man-months, person-days, or hours, it is always difficult to be certain. Traditional methods (specifically, those that produce lengthy detailed project schedules up front) try to address this uncertainty by spending more and more time and effort to become ... well, more certain. In agile development, estimations are recognized as just that—estimations. We can take them for what they are worth, or we can try to get more precise by spending time and money to plan. In the end, we often discover that, having spent the time to be precise, the requirements and needs change anyway, invalidating our work and wasting our time.

When scoping a backlog in agile development, you will find yourself working in probabilities rather than certainties. Essentially, there are a couple of different ways of determining the scope of the Release Backlog. Starting with estimations, your Product Backlog will be in

- T-shirt sizes—if you do not have Scrum teams yet, or your Scrum teams have not established a velocity, you will probably use T-shirt sizing, which will yield man-weeks or man-months.
- Story points—if you have functioning Scrum teams, they will have estimated the backlog in story points.

Likewise, your teams are measurable in one or both of two ways:

- Person/time (like man-months or person-days)—if your Scrum teams are not yet established.
- Story point velocity—if your Scrum teams are functioning for more than three Sprints, they will have a measurable and somewhat consistent velocity (a rough average number of story points per Sprint).

This means that if your Scrum teams have not yet been formed, you can determine the rough scope of your Release Backlog in terms of either a fixed timeframe or a fixed scope. In other words, if we know that we have

400 man-months of human resource that we can spend over 10 months, all we have to do is walk through the Product Backlog, from the top, until we accumulate work roughly equal to 400 man-months. On the other hand, if we have 40 man-months per month of human resource and we want to complete a specific list of items from the Product Backlog that add up to 600 man-months, we know that we will need roughly 600/40 months, or 15 months.

On the other hand, if you have functioning Scrum teams that have sized the Product Backlog and have established velocities, you can do calculations similar to those in the previous paragraphs, but in story points instead of man-months. In the fixed-timeframe case, if you had 10 months and your Scrum teams had a total velocity of 75 story points per Sprint, you would be able to scope in roughly 750 story points worth of backlog items. In the fixed-scope case, if you wanted to get 500 story points done and your Scrum teams had a total velocity of 50 story points, you should expect to be able to complete the 500 points from the backlog in about five Sprints.

Regardless of the method you use, you will find that your Release Backlog is all about probabilities. Many organizations look at their Release Backlog like this (see Figure 3.2):

- The top 50% of the Release Backlog has a very high probability of completion.
- The next 25% of the Release Backlog has a moderate probability of completion.
- The bottom 25% of the Release Backlog has a very low probability of completion.

Now, while this sounds downright sacrilegious to traditional methods of scoping and committing (no matter what), there are some important points that should be considered. First, in any traditional "waterfall" project, there is frequently some degree of shifting of dates or modification of scope caused by overcommitment in the project. Agile development suffers from the same problem—we also can easily overcommit in an agile project. However, we can discover the extent of our overcommitment faster, and we can soften that impact over time. First, as each Sprint is completed, the Release Backlog gets smaller, and our Scrum teams' velocity and predictability tend to improve. Accordingly, it is much easier to see what portion of the Release Backlog will be finished at the end of the project and that visibility will improve as the project

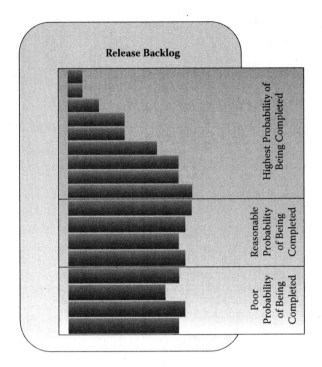

FIGURE 3.2
Release Backlog whose items in the top 50% have the highest probability for completion.

progresses. We can leverage this pattern by making sure that the portion of the scope that we *must* get done is at least in the top 50% of the Release Backlog.

And, of course, adjustments can and will be made on a Sprint-by-Sprint basis as the Scrum teams actually complete items and remove them from the backlog and as experienced Scrum teams and Product Owners slice backlog items into smaller and smaller pieces, removing the less-valuable pieces from the Release Backlog as the project progresses.

The biggest challenge, of course, is how we choose to communicate our planning to our customer. Do we make the same old mistake and commit to both content and timeframe? Or, do we set the number of Sprints and complete as much as we can in those Sprints? In my efforts with agile projects, my customers are usually trying to overcome an inability to get the necessary value done in a predictable timeframe. When we turn to an agile project, set the date, and then focus our Scrum teams on the value that we need to achieve, the projects end on time. I coach them to be as visible with their customers as is reasonable[1] and update their customers after every one to three Sprints (depending on the length of the project) regarding the condition of the Release Backlog and the state of the "must-haves" in the Release Backlog. Yes, we cut scope as we go, but we keep to the must-haves through effective user story slicing and a clear focus on what is valuable and what is not valuable during the project.

SETTING THE SPRINT SCHEDULE

When using Scrum, you will want to establish some parameters around Sprint length and Sprint scheduling. With regard to Sprint length, my recommendation for most organizations (experienced or beginners) is to go with Sprints 2 or 3 that are weeks long. While Scrum also allows for 1-week, 4-weeks, and 1-month Sprints (Scrum only *suggests* that Sprints should not exceed 1 month; you could set up a 12-day Sprint if you really wanted to), the shorter Sprint length allows organizations to learn faster. Smaller Sprints require less planning and provide more opportunities to learn. If you are at all familiar with genetic research, you might have run across the geneticists' friend: the fruit fly. The fruit fly has a very short life span, enabling the geneticist to examine multiple generations in a relatively short period of time (a generation takes about 10 days). Short Sprints have the same impact on organizations—they allow for rapid learning and experimentation through the frequent repetition of the complete development process, from planning and analysis to coding and testing.

In addition, you will want to set your Sprints to be of consistent length. Whether you choose 1 month or 2 weeks—stay with it. Much of the predictability of your Scrum teams (and thus your ability to predict when a feature or a project will be finished) relies on consistent iteration lengths to create a baseline time box for the Scrum teams. This does not mean that all teams need to have the same Sprint length. However, whatever length your Scrum teams go with—do not change it unless you have to, and if you do, do so as rarely as possible.

The last issue with regard to the Sprint schedule is the applicability of the schedule to your Scrum teams. In other words, will all of your Scrum teams use the same schedule, or will each team be allowed to set its own Sprint schedule? You will find that optimum Sprint length is not a one-size-fits-all situation, even if you do decide to have all teams comply with the same schedule. In my opinion, however, it is better to have all of the teams on the same project share the same Sprint schedule. This makes project reporting a bit easier, allowing you to generate detailed and highly accurate reports at the end of each iteration. At the same time, if you happen to be a Product Owner and all of your three Scrum teams are going into Sprint Planning on the same day, you could have a problem being in multiple places at the same time. An alternative is to stagger the Sprint (for example, some of the teams might start on Monday, and the rest of the teams begin on Tuesday).[2] This gives your Product Owner a little more time to meet with all three teams during Sprint Planning.

If you are at the point at which you are ready to flip a coin on this one, let me ease the problem—go with synchronized 2-week Sprints. This will create a rapid learning cycle, a consistent time box, easy reporting, and a relatively simple problem to solve for your Product Owners; since Sprint Planning for a 2-week Sprint is generally not more than 4 hours, a Product Owner can easily attend two Sprint Planning meetings in 1 day and likely could attend most of three Sprint Planning meetings in 1 day with little difficulty.

STAFFING OF SCRUM TEAMS

The fundamental definition of a Scrum team is that it has the skills it needs to get the job done. To that end, before you start a new project, it is a good time to (a) check the skills on the teams you have and (b) build new teams based on the skills that you need. This can be a difficult process, as you will also want to consider some of the following when you make your decisions:

- Who works well with whom? As much as we would like everyone to behave as adults in the professional world, well … it just does not always happen. For whatever reason, there are people that work well together, and there are people who do not work well together. It is not a good idea to put people who do not work well together on a Scrum team unless you believe they can be taught, at least, to be tolerant of one another. You are, however, going to run into people who cannot be put into the same team together, much less the same organization. My advice: Don't try. There is too much a Scrum team can accomplish; do not start the team out with a huge problem to fix.
- What are the individual career goals of each individual? Employees are also people. They have goals. They have, in most cases, a direction that they want their career to go. If you are a good enough leader to

ask your employees what it is they want to do in 3 years or 5 years (and many of us managers may or may not be good leaders, but our company requires that we ask these questions once a year anyway), you then do not want to ignore what your employee tells you when it comes to staffing Scrum teams. Sometimes, you will need to put someone on the team for the skills you want them to learn rather than the skills they already possess.

- How much am I willing to put the right people together and do the technical training on the job? Any time you are staffing a position, there is a balance of technical skills and interpersonal skills that must be considered. When you are building a Scrum team, this decision becomes a thousand times more important; you are expecting the team members to collaborate, to work closely together day after day. So, who would you hire? The perfect team member who lacks the skill to write Java code or the perfect Java developer who has the interpersonal skills of a rock? Answering this question will help you better understand how to make decisions when the choices are not so clear.
- Am I building component teams or feature teams? Component teams focus on specific modules or "components" within the product. Feature teams are brought together to build complete features in the product. Component teams require coders, testers, analysts, and so on with a similar technical knowledge of the product (e.g., teams that build protocol stacks and converters or focus on specific middleware or architectural capabilities). Feature teams require a similar *functional* knowledge of the product and often a much broader set of development skills (including documentation, database, and architectural).

When you already have Scrum teams, but you are considering making changes to put the right skills in the "right place," you should also consider the "teamwork" component of your team's velocity. Teams are intact complex entities; they subsume the personalities, strengths, and weaknesses of their members and become something new. You cannot take a member off a team, or replace a team member, without ostensibly creating a new team and, in fact, starting that team over. Therefore, when you move personnel from one team to another, you are actually "resetting" two teams—the team that gave up the team member and the team that got the new team member. Of course, if the team you have right now is performing poorly, creating a whole new team might be exactly what is needed.

It is also worth noting that some organizations subscribe to the idea that people on high-performing teams can be used to "seed" new teams to create more high-performing teams. This idea is absolute nonsense. A high-performing team performs the way it does because of the unique combination of personalities, skills, strengths, weaknesses, and investment that was brought together to create the team. When you remove individuals from the team (or split the team into two parts to create two new teams), the odds of creating more high-performing teams are no better than the odds of the first team becoming high performing. When the original team is split to seed two more, two completely new teams are created, and one high-performing team is destroyed.

TRAINING OF SCRUM TEAMS

The beginning of a project is an excellent time to get any necessary training out of the way. It may come in the form of self-study, book study groups, classroom, or Web-based training. However you do it, this is the time to consider what needs to be done. There are several different categories of training you may want to consider. Here are a few:

- **Process retraining.** Does everyone on the project understand the organizational processes and procedures? Have there been changes that teams should be aware of? Does the project itself have unusual or different process requirements that other projects might not have? It is worth a little retraining to make sure that everyone is starting from the same place with regard to process requirements.
- **Product training.** Does everyone on the project understand the product and the goals of the release? Do they understand the marketplace and the competition's entries? Do not assume they do and, most important, do not expect a kickoff meeting to answer all of the relevant questions.
- **Scrum training.** In addition to new hires who may not have gotten the training the last time around, teams can get into bad habits. By doing a little retraining at the beginning of the project, some teams might get a fresh start.
- **Tools training.** Have you changed any tools since the previous project began? If so, is everyone up on the latest instructions?

Put together a schedule for training and try to get it all done before or during the first Sprint of the project. This will get your teams off to a good start with fewer misunderstandings and misinterpretations during the project.

REVIEW/REVISE DONENESS DEFINITION

The DONEness definition[3] is a common artifact used by many agile development organizations. It defines the list of things that must be true for a backlog item to be considered finished. The entire concept is to accomplish two things: (a) get everyone talking about being "done" and meaning the same thing and (b) ensure that all Scrum teams achieve a high level of quality with all backlog items. Most DONEness definitions begin with these two items:

1. The backlog item achieves the value desired by the Product Owner.
2. Nothing else breaks because of the changes.

Then, the list may have things on it like the following:

- All unit tests pass.
- All acceptance tests pass.
- All source code and test code are properly checked in.
- All coding and naming standards have been properly followed.
- All design pattern standards have been properly followed.
- All related functional specifications have been updated.
- All related design specifications have been updated.

Depending on the organization, the product, and the statuatory or regulatory requirements, the list can become long.

Regardless of length, DONEness is not a static state. From project to project, DONEness can be different. Documents or coding standards required in some projects may be different in others. Before starting any project, it is a good idea to look at your current definition of DONEness and decide if it still makes sense for the upcoming project.

CREATION (OR UPDATING) OF THE ARCHITECTURE DEFINITION

It is absolutely imperative that a product development effort be accompanied by a defined architecture. This is important not only to ensure that the product can meet the various system constraints to which it must conform to (running on certain platforms, supporting a maximum number of concurrent users, etc.), but also to create a shared vision of how the product code is supposed to be structured (i.e., what will the architecture support vs. what the application functionality will have to provide). Without a clear definition, Scrum teams frequently find themselves unable to make important decisions about technical solutions.

The architecture definition should define how all of the known system constraints are to be addressed before the product development begins. What is the platform? What languages can be used? How are users managed? Where and how are application data stored? How is the data managed and accessed? At some point, the definition becomes more practical, for example, when the architecture provides a queuing and printing subsystem so that none of the application functionality will have to write its own.

It is also important to note that the application architecture should be defined before the construction of the application functionality begins. How pieces of the application interface and communicate with other pieces of the application can spell the difference between an easily testable application and one that is extraordinarily difficult to test (a difference that could become measured in thousands, if not tens of thousands, of dollars in very short order). Modules that are more directly coupled with other modules become increasingly difficult to test.

Of course, any architecture definition is subject to change. As the project begins and the Scrum teams are building "just enough" architecture to support the features they have committed to build, it is extremely likely that the architecture definition will undergo change. This is not only normal but also should be expected in the initial releases of an application. Architecture definitions are not written in stone; they should be used as a guideline for ongoing development and be modified and updated as necessary during the actual development effort.

GROOMING FOR THE FIRST SPRINT

Backlog grooming, explained in the next section, can be described simply as "priming the pump." To successfully complete Sprint Planning, Scrum teams need backlog items that are small and well understood. During most Sprints of a project, the teams groom in one Sprint work they will likely do in the next Sprint. However, when starting a new project, you will only have two choices, depending on whether you already have Scrum teams engaged in a project.

1. If you have Scrum teams already active and in a project, they can begin grooming the new Release Backlog as they wrap up the project they are currently engaged in, or
2. You can hold a few backlog grooming workshops prior to starting the new project. Remember, though, if you do grooming workshops, you want to keep the workshops to no more than 2 hours with 30 minutes or so between sessions (grooming is a difficult and detailed process; it is best to keep everyone as fresh as possible).

When grooming the backlog, you do not want your teams grooming more than one or two Sprints worth of work, so it should not take more than 2 or 3 days to get the backlog into a "ready" state. And, of course, the shorter the Sprint, the less time it will take to get ready.

Preparatory grooming is one of the last steps you will want to take prior to starting your project. As with any grooming, the later it is done, the less likely it is that there will be any need to rework or reanalyze the groomed backlog items.

REFERENCE

Schiel, James A. 2010. *Enterprise-Scale Agile Software Development*. Boca Raton, FL: CRC Press.

ENDNOTES

1. Of course, with some customers, too much visibility can be a bad thing. You will need to determine how much your customer needs to know. Try to be straight with your customer—no matter who they are. If their "pet" feature is in the bottom 50% of the backlog, the sooner they know there is a risk, the sooner you can reach some kind of a compromise. This is one of the reasons, in fact, that I recommend short release cycles. With a short release, if you cannot complete something in one release, it will not be long before you can do it in another.

2. Schiel, *Enterprise-Scale*, 222–224.

3. Ibid., 213–217.

4

Backlog Grooming

INTRODUCTION

The backlog grooming workshop (what some call the "pre-Sprint analysis") is intended to help the Scrum team simplify the backlog prior to Sprint Planning by discussing the stories that are "next up" on the Product Backlog and understanding them well enough to slice them into smaller, simpler, and less-risky backlog items. For example, a backlog item that adds a customer registration function to our product might be easily sliced into three items that (a) collect the customer's name, (b) collect the customer's address, and (c) collect the customer's preferences. Each of these three smaller backlog items is simpler, less risky, easier to estimate, and an excellent size for a Sprint. The new, smaller backlog items are then estimated by the team, and the "parent" item is removed from the Product Backlog (Figure 4.1).

Backlog grooming also provides an opportunity to estimate items on the Product Backlog that are new and might not yet have an effort estimate. In this chapter, we explore how to plan and facilitate backlog grooming workshops and how to estimate backlog items.

Last, in the previous chapter on release planning, I kept the discussion high level (release planning is a book all by itself). In this chapter and the several that follow, you will find a much more detailed discussion of the meeting and its purpose, as well as how to

- Prepare for the meeting
- Set up for the meeting
- Facilitate the meeting, and
- Wrap up the meeting

FIGURE 4.1
Inputs and outputs of the backlog grooming meeting.

It is all of these instructions that I believe provide the true "practical" use of Scrum. However, at the same time, please be aware that Scrum provides little information about how the meetings and workshops discussed in the following chapters are actually supposed to be held. Therefore, nearly all of the information you will find in these chapters is provided from my own experiences using Scrum. What this means, of course, is that you can start with the instructions I provide and then modify as you see fit (as long as your meetings provide the same output or outputs as required by Scrum or as documented herein).

PREPARING FOR THE BACKLOG GROOMING WORKSHOP

Backlog grooming workshops are usually short meetings held during the Sprint. Some teams accomplish the same thing with "preplanning meetings" during 1 day near the end of the Sprint, but I have found that this practice tends to do more to upset the Scrum team, which, during the end of the Sprint, wants to concentrate on finishing the Sprint and is reluctant to engage in long meetings with a different focus. My other objection to the "preplanning day" at the end of the Sprint is that backlog grooming can be an arduous process. Asking a team to do it for an entire day frequently ensures lower-quality work.

I recommend holding backlog grooming workshops in 90-minute increments once or twice during each week of the Sprint. For instance, you could hold the workshops on Tuesday and Thursday afternoons from 1 p.m. to 2:30 p.m. Since the goal of backlog grooming is to prepare enough backlog items for the next Sprint, teams that can effectively slice and estimate backlog items quickly may find themselves able to hold only one backlog grooming meeting per week, instead of two. As with the daily Scrum, however, whenever it is you schedule the workshops and at whatever frequency you schedule them, keep it consistent.

Also, send an invitation to all team members (including the Product Owner and any additional stakeholders who wish to be at the workshop) at the beginning of the Sprint so that all backlog grooming meetings are on their calendar. Even if you end up not needing all of the meetings, it is far easier to cancel a scheduled meeting than it is to schedule a new meeting at the last minute.

SETTING UP THE BACKLOG GROOMING WORKSHOP

Properly setting up a backlog grooming workshop is the key to making each meeting a consistently effective meeting. When you hold a grooming workshop, you need the following:

- a conference room or the team room
- a central table (with or without chairs)
- flip charts or whiteboards
- a digital camera to capture work from whiteboards and flip charts
- previously estimated backlog items, on index cards, sorted by story point size
- Post-it notes, markers, whiteboard markers
- A laptop or desktop computer to access the backlog management tool (if applicable)
- Backlog items that need to be sliced or estimated (preferably on cards). This list would be made up of (a) any backlog items on the Product Backlog that currently have no effort estimates and (b) backlog items

on the top of the Product Backlog that are too big to fit into the Sprint. For many teams, these are backlog items that have a story point size of greater than 3; in general, though, these are backlog items that would take two or three people on the team more than 1 week to complete.

To prepare the environment for the meeting, follow these steps:

1. Clear the table. Other materials on the table can be distracting.
2. Put the Post-its on the table with markers (make sure that the markers work).
3. Put the whiteboard markers with the whiteboard (also make sure these markers work).
4. Put the previously estimated backlog item cards on the table in stacks of similar size cards (e.g., a stack of 1-point items, a stack of 2-point items, etc.).
5. If there is a backlog management tool in use, get the laptop or desktop signed on to the tool so that backlog items can be reviewed as needed.
6. Put the items that need to be sliced or estimated on the table where the Product Owner will sit. The order of the stack is as follows: unestimated items in Product Backlog priority order and then items that need to be sliced for the next Sprint, also in Product Backlog priority order.
7. Start the meeting on time.

FACILITATING THE BACKLOG GROOMING WORKSHOP

When facilitating the backlog grooming workshop, your job is to keep the team focused, on task, and completing the slicing and estimating of as many backlog items as possible in the time allotted. Essentially, the flow of the meeting is as follows:

1. Discuss the top backlog item on the stack of items to be sliced or estimated.
2. The Product Owner drives this conversation, with the team asking clarifying questions. Encourage the use of flip chart pages or the whiteboard to clarify concepts. Whenever notes or other drawings are created on a flip chart page or on the whiteboard, make sure to

include the ID of the backlog item on the drawing somewhere. Take pictures of whiteboard drawings before they are erased.

a. If the item is an unestimated item, the team asks enough questions to gain a clearer understanding of the item and then provides an estimate for the item.

b. If the item is to be sliced, the team asks enough questions to slice the item into smaller backlog items. The resulting backlog items are then discussed and estimated. Any items estimated to be larger than 3 story points are put back on the stack of items to be sliced and estimated. Items estimated at 3 story points or less are considered "ready" for the next Sprint.

3. Go back to step 1 and repeat process until

a. There are no more unestimated stories on the backlog, and there are enough backlog items on the top of the Product Backlog that are 3 story points or less in size and add up to at least 125% of the team's current velocity, *or*

b. The 90 minutes are up.

When either of the completion conditions is met, the meeting is over.

WRAPPING UP THE BACKLOG GROOMING WORKSHOP

Collect all flip chart pages (make sure each page is identified with the ID of the backlog item referred to in the page) and take digital pictures of the flip chart page (save the actual page for later, just in case it is needed). If applicable, update your backlog management tool by adding estimations, by creating new backlog items (usually by slicing existing backlog items), and by attaching pictures of flip chart pages and whiteboard drawings to the proper backlog items.

5

The Sprint Planning Meeting

INTRODUCTION

The focus of the Sprint Planning meeting is to allow the Scrum team to determine the content of the Sprint. This is accomplished by discussing the highest-priority backlog item, getting a clear idea of what the Product Owner wants from the backlog item, and then reducing the backlog item to a series of tasks that must be completed for the team to properly build the item. For this process to be successfully completed, the ScrumMaster not only will want to be properly prepared but also should have a good plan for facilitating the meeting. That is what this chapter discusses (Figure 5.1).

PREPARING FOR THE SPRINT PLANNING MEETING

The length of the Sprint Planning meeting is directly impacted by the length of the Sprint. For a Sprint that is up to 2 weeks long, you should expect a Sprint Planning meeting of 3 or 4 hours. When the Sprint is 3 or 4 weeks or a full calendar month, Sprint Planning should take up to 8 hours. The difficult part, however, is determining the type of planning meeting you will want to schedule. There are several valid versions, depending on whether the team is colocated or scattered in two or more geographically separated locations. Teams that are colocated tend to do fine with a single meeting. Teams that are not colocated (and even some teams that are colocated) will often request that the planning meeting be held in two pieces.

The first part of the planning meeting is used to identify the backlog items that the team is likely to commit to for the upcoming Sprint. The items are discussed with the Product Owner until the team is comfortable

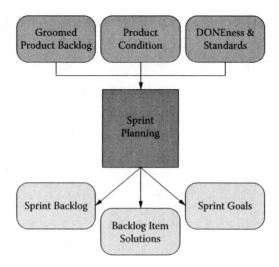

FIGURE 5.1
Inputs and outputs of the Sprint Planning meeting.

with each one. Then, the teams will split up into smaller groups, discuss a solution for the backlog items, and come back to a second planning meeting to discuss their solution and resulting tasks with the rest of the team.

You should plan to invite the entire Scrum team (including the Product Owner) as well as any interested stakeholders and managers to the meeting (or meetings, if necessary). If possible, hold the meetings in the team room, but if necessary, a conference room will suffice.

SETTING UP THE SPRINT PLANNING MEETING

Setting up for the planning meeting is similar to setting up for the backlog grooming workshop, as the activities are also similar.

For a Single-Part Planning Meeting

- a conference room or the team room
- a central table (with or without chairs)
- flip charts or whiteboards
- a digital camera to capture work from whiteboards and flip charts
- "Sprint-size" backlog items, on index cards, sorted by Product Backlog priority

- Post-it notes, markers, whiteboard markers
- A laptop or desktop computer to access the backlog management tool (if applicable)

To prepare the environment for the meeting, follow these steps:

1. Clear the table. Other materials on the table can be distracting.
2. Put the Post-its on the table with markers (make sure that the markers work).
3. Put the whiteboard markers with the whiteboard (also make sure these markers work).
4. If there is a backlog management tool in use, get the laptop or desktop signed on to the tool so that backlog items can be reviewed as needed.
5. Put the items that need to be sliced or estimated on the table where the Product Owner will sit. The order of the stack is as follows: unestimated items in Product Backlog priority order and then items that need to be sliced for the next Sprint, also in Product Backlog priority order.
6. Start the meeting on time.

If the meeting is to be held in two parts and everyone is colocated, let the team members take what they need (flip chart pages, easels, markers, etc.). When everyone comes back together, they can bring all of the materials back with them.

For Multipart Planning Meetings

If the meeting is being held in two parts across more than one location, you will need to ensure that all sites are properly prepared for their part of the meeting. In this situation, you will need to prepare the following for each site:

- A conference room or private space at each location
- A monitor or data projector and screen, software, and personal computer (PC) or Mac to view what is being discussed at the two or more locations of the meeting. Software like iChat,[1] Skype,[2] Oovoo,[3] GoToMeeting,[4] WebEx,[5] and Windows Live Messenger[6] have some or all of the requisite features needed to support the collaborative nature of the planning meeting.

- In my experience, many teleconferencing meetings are weakened or even ended by bad audio quality, so be particularly careful here. At sites where employees work alone, a headset and microphone connection is best. At sites where multiple people will be gathering together in a room, use conferencing equipment that provides good audio quality (Polycom[7] is my favorite).

To prepare for the meeting, do the following[8]:

1. Make sure that the meeting announcement includes all of the information necessary for everyone to get connected. Encourage those who are doing this for the first time to do a "test run" before the planning meeting to ensure that they have the software they need to join the meeting.
2. Make sure that someone (usually the ScrumMaster or the Product Owner) has direct access to the Product Backlog and can display backlog items on the laptop or desktop display such that others on the call will be able to see the backlog item description as it is discussed.
3. Make sure that everyone on the meeting is able to take advantage of the whiteboarding capabilities of the teleconferencing software you have chosen to use. Do not just put the team in a meeting without some kind of introduction to how to use all of the functions of the software properly.
4. Start the meeting on time.

FACILITATING THE SPRINT PLANNING MEETING

Facilitating a Sprint Planning meeting is similar to facilitating a backlog grooming meeting, but there is a little more to it. Why? Because backlog grooming is about preparing the Product Backlog; however, Sprint Planning is part of one of the "inspect-and-adapt" feedback loops in Scrum. That makes it important to do properly and effectively. An ineffective or poorly run Sprint Planning meeting can really ruin a Sprint. We will look at facilitating Sprint Planning both as a single meeting and as a meeting in two parts.

For Single-Part Planning Meetings ("Commitment-Based Planning")

1. First, you will want to establish what the team believes they can commit to in the upcoming Sprint. One of the ways to accomplish this is to do the following:

   a. Ask the team the following question: "In your opinion, was the result of the previous Sprint easy to achieve, exactly what the team should achieve, or too difficult to achieve again?" Get everyone's thoughts and discuss the answers. In general, what you want to find out is whether the team's effort during the previous Sprint can be easily repeated.

   b. Discuss the backlog items completed in the previous Sprint with the team. Were any of the items almost finished when the Sprint began? As a result, does the team feel like their commitment this Sprint should be less than what was achieved in the previous Sprint or more?

   c. Poll the team for any vacations, training sessions, department meetings, or any other absences expected during the upcoming Sprint. Compared to the previous Sprint, is this more or less?

2. Use the results of these questions to help the team determine what they are willing to commit to in the upcoming Sprint. If the answers lead the team to believe that they can get more done in the upcoming Sprint, they should commit to more work in this Sprint than in the previous Sprint. Otherwise, the team should commit to the same amount or less. Let us look at a few examples:

   a. In the previous Sprint, the team completed 25 story points worth of work. They did not have to work hard to achieve the 25 points because 8 of them came from the prior Sprint and were finished within the first couple days. After discussion with the team, there are no special meetings, vacations, or training sessions planned during the current Sprint. The team decides to commit to somewhere between 17 and 18 story points in the current Sprint.

   b. In the previous Sprint, the team completed 27 story points worth of work. It was a little bit of a stretch because there was a conference coming up, and the sales department wanted to get a version of the product under development with a particular feature in it. With July approaching, the team reported four members taking a week of vacation. After some discussion, the team decided that, without the stretch work in the previous Sprint, the velocity would have been 23 instead of 27. With the planned vacations, the team feels that their velocity would be cut in half. So, the team decides to commit to 12 story points in the current Sprint.

3. With a "target" commitment determined, you can then move to discuss the highest priority on the Product Backlog. This backlog item should be small and somewhat clearly defined (through backlog grooming) when it is discussed in Sprint Planning. However, if the item is considered by the team to be too big or too complex, they may slice and reestimate the backlog item before discussing it. Usually, a good size for a backlog item is something that can be completed by two or three people on the team in less than a week. So, with a "right-size" backlog item, we then do the following:

   a. Discuss the backlog item with the Product Owner to determine the "agreement." This part is so important, I have included it as a separate chapter in this book, Chapter 9, "Creating Backlog Agreements."

   b. With the backlog item well understood, the team then determines a solution for the backlog item. This might involve discussion of database changes, architectural changes, test requirements, and user interface changes (to say the least). The team determines the nature of the solution and the impact of the solution. You should expect drawings and other facts to come out during the discussion, all of which should be captured on whiteboards or flip chart pages.[9]

   I have found, in many planning meetings, that this part of the meeting is either very productive or *extremely* unproductive. In the unproductive case, I see people who are not directly involved in the backlog item conversation just kind of wasting time doodling or checking e-mails; they may even leave the meeting and come back. It is important to keep everyone "fully functional and productive." Therefore, during this part of the meeting, you may find it more effective actually to discuss two backlog items and then have the team split[10] into two subteams. Each subteam is then given 1 hour to determine a solution and create a list of task. After 1 hour, both subteams come back together and review their solutions and task lists looking for feedback, which is immediately incorporated into the final decision. If the team is able to do more work, you repeat the process, discussing two backlog items instead of one, and then creating the solutions and tasks separately, coming back together after an hour to do a team review of the outcomes.

c. Once the solution has been agreed on, the team can then create the tasks necessary to accomplish the solution. Be careful that your tasks do not represent waterfall development concepts, however. In other words, avoid tasks like "analyze database changes," "design database changes," "change the database," and so on. Tasks that say things like "analyze," "design," "code," and "test" tend to create noncollaborative behaviors and reintroduce the waterfall into the Sprint. Instead, you want your tasks to focus on actual functionality, like "build the screen" or "create the join process." These kinds of tasks encourage collaboration across team members, who can then work together to figure out how to "test the join process," "document the join process," and "code the join process." Each task is estimated in the number of hours that the team agrees the task will take. In general, the size of a task should be no greater than 16 hours. However, should the team be unable to create an arrangement of tasks less than 16 hours, it is also not considered important enough to waste more than a few minutes trying to create more, smaller tasks. Finally, it is generally considered best practice not to assign tasks to a team member during Sprint Planning and to allow task assignment to occur as appropriate during the Sprint. Still, some teams do assign tasks during Sprint Planning—neither practice is wrong or right, though I would advise leaving task assignment for during the Sprint when the tasks *need* to be assigned, unless, of course, there is only one person on the team with the skills to do the task; you almost have to under these conditions to ensure that the team does not overcommit through its skills bottleneck.

d. Having created a solution for the backlog item and both created and estimated the tasks necessary to build the solution, the team should take a quick look at the new "size" of the backlog item (as represented by the total task size) and the story point size of the backlog item. If there is more than a small discrepancy, the team should correct the story point size of the backlog item.

4. The team now reviews the total effort added to the Sprint Backlog, in terms of tasks and overall work, and decides if they are able to do

more work than what has been listed so far. Part of the team's consideration at this point should be the number of story points of work that they believe they can commit to during the Sprint. The other part of what the team should consider is what many might call "gut feel." Does the total workload "feel" like it might be too much? Too little? Granted, this is subjective, and the very concept of using one's feelings to make a decision like this may fly in the face of the metrics and statistics we tend to employ, but it is best to keep this subjective aspect so that the team knows that the final decision with regard to how much work they commit to is theirs and no one else's. Anything less takes away the team's responsibility to self-manage.

For example, many teams I have worked with that are uncomfortable with this concept tend to use their "capacity," calculated by adding up all of their available hours, to figure out how much work they are actually able to do during a Sprint. This makes them more comfortable than a "feeling" because, well, the math cannot be wrong. Then, they perform one or two Sprints, constantly discovering that they are committing to far more work than they can actually do (for example, they calculate their capacity at 950 hours, load the Sprint with 945 hours of tasks, and find themselves able to complete only about 820 hours). After looking for an answer to this obvious inefficiency of the team (that is, where does the 125 hours keep going?), they decide that it is clearly their task estimation that is causing the problem, and they begin analyzing their actual hours against their task estimation hours. They discover differences between the actuals and the estimates (not enough to account for the whole 125 hours, mind you) and take steps to fix these differences. Unfortunately, the effort to analyze the tasks costs 50 hours and the effort to create "better" task estimates costs 2 more hours of work during the Sprint Planning. Note, however, how much *more* work is getting done during the Sprint. At best, no more work is getting done, despite the "improved" task estimates, and at worst, at least 52 hours of work time has been taken away due to this effort to improve the task estimates. The bottom line—it is better to let the team decide what they can and cannot do by using their own history (velocity) and their own gut feeling for what can and what cannot be done. If the team feels that they can do more in this Sprint, you repeat the discussion/solutioning process with the next-highest-priority item on the Product Backlog.

If the team feels that they can do no more backlog items in the Sprint, Sprint Planning is over. The team has completed their dual task of creating a commitment for the Product Owner regarding what will be built during the Sprint, and they have created the Sprint Backlog that operationally documents their commitment.

For Two-Part Planning Meetings ("Velocity-Based Planning")

1. First for two-part planning, you will want to establish what the team believes they can commit to in the upcoming Sprint. Follow the same instructions provided for the single-part planning meeting in this chapter.
2. Use the results of these questions to help the team determine what they are willing to commit to in the upcoming Sprint. If the answers lead the team to believe that they can get more done in the upcoming Sprint, they should commit to more work in this Sprint than in the previous Sprint. Otherwise, they should commit to the same amount or less as described in the discussion of the single-part planning meeting in this chapter.
3. With a "target" commitment determined, the team turns attention to identifying the backlog items on the Product Backlog that will be built during the Sprint. In general, this is not a difficult effort, simply accumulating story point sizes until the target size is met (or even slightly exceeded). Sometimes, it may be necessary to reorder some of the backlog items on the Product Backlog to ensure that the right-size backlog item appears at the top of the backlog at the right time (in other words, it may be desirable to swap a 3-point item for a 1-point item because the 1-point item fits better into the Sprint). For each identified backlog item, the team discusses the backlog item with the Product Owner to determine the agreement.
4. Once the proper backlog items have been identified, the first part of the meeting ends.
5. The second part of the meeting is all about turning the selected backlog items into a Sprint Backlog. This is performed by doing the following:
   a. With the backlog item well understood, the team then determines a solution for the backlog item. This might involve discussion of database changes, architectural changes, test requirements, and UI changes (to say the least). The team determines the nature and the impact of the solution. You should expect drawings and other

facts to come out during the discussion, all of which should be captured on whiteboards or flip chart pages.[11]

b. Once the solution has been agreed on, the team can then create the tasks necessary to accomplish the solution. Be careful that your tasks do not represent waterfall development concepts, however.

c. Having created a solution for the backlog item and both created and estimated the tasks necessary to build the solution, the team should take a quick look at the new "size" of the backlog item (as represented by the total task size) and the story point size of the backlog item. If there is more than a small discrepancy, the team should correct the story point size of the backlog item.

6. If the team has reached their velocity goal, Sprint Planning is over. The team has completed the dual task of creating a commitment for the Product Owner regarding what will be built during the Sprint and has created the Sprint Backlog that operationally documents their commitment.

For Two-Part Noncolocated Planning Meetings

This approach works well when your team is divided across multiple geographic locations and holding a full-day Sprint Planning is prohibitive. (As a case in point, one of my customers has teams with members in New York, Los Angeles, and Bangalore, India, which gives the team a 12.5-hour difference as a result of the time zones. Imagine trying to hold a 6-hour meeting. When would you hold it that did not make it part of the middle of somebody's nighttime?) Basically, we hold the beginning of the Sprint Planning meeting to identify the backlog items, give the teams time to work in their respective locations, and then reconvene to complete the planning.

1. First, you will want to establish what the team believes they can commit to in the upcoming Sprint. Follow the same instructions provided for the single-part planning meeting discussed in this chapter.

2. Use the results of these questions to help the team determine what they are willing to commit to in the upcoming Sprint. If the answers lead the team to believe that they can get more done in the upcoming Sprint, they should commit to more work in this Sprint than in the previous Sprint. Otherwise, they should commit to the same amount

or less (look at the discussion for the single-part planning meeting in this chapter for examples).

3. With a "target" commitment determined, the team turns attention to identifying the backlog items on the Product Backlog that will be built during the Sprint. In general, this is not a difficult effort, simply accumulating story point sizes until the target size is met (or even slightly exceeded). Sometimes, it may be necessary to reorder some of the backlog items on the Product Backlog to ensure that the right-size backlog item appears at the top of the backlog at the right time (in other words, it may be desirable to swap a 3-point item for a 1-point item because the 1-point item fits better into the Sprint). For each identified backlog item, the team discusses the backlog item with the Product Owner to determine the agreement.

4. Once the proper backlog items have been identified, the first part of the meeting ends. Team members then, working from their respective locations, continue the work independently by doing the following:

   a. Each subteam then determines a solution for the backlog item. This might involve discussion of database changes, architectural changes, test requirements, and user-interface changes (to say the least). The subteam determines the nature and the impact of the solution. You should expect drawings and other facts to come out during the discussion, all of which should be captured on whiteboards or flip chart pages.[12]

   b. Once the solution has been agreed on, the subteam can then create the tasks necessary to accomplish the solution. Be careful that your tasks do not represent waterfall development concepts, however (look at the discussion for the single-part planning meeting in this chapter for more information).

   c. Having created a solution for the backlog item and both created and estimated the tasks necessary to build the solution, the subteam should take a quick look at the new size of the backlog item (as represented by the total task size) and the story point size of the backlog item. If there is more than a small discrepancy, the subteam should correct the story point size of the backlog item.

5. The team comes back together at its earliest convenience and reviews the solutions and tasks created by the subteams. Feedback is immediately incorporated into the solutions and task lists, and the team finalizes its commitment to the Product Owner.

WRAPPING UP THE SPRINT PLANNING MEETING

Once the solutions and task list are completed, collect all flip chart pages (make sure each page is identified with the ID of the backlog item to which the content of the page refers) and take digital pictures of the flip chart page (save the actual page for later, just in case it is needed). If applicable, update your backlog management tool by adding tasks and estimations, by creating new backlog items (usually by slicing existing backlog items), and by attaching pictures of flip chart pages and whiteboard drawings to the proper backlog items.

ENDNOTES

1. Go to http://www.apple.com/findouthow/mac/#ichatbasics for more information.
2. Go to http://www.skype.com/intl/en-us/welcomeback/ for more information.
3. Go to http://www.oovoo.com/home.aspx for more information.
4. Go to http://www.gotomeeting.com/ for more information.
5. Go to http://www.webex.com/ for more information.
6. Go to http://explore.live.com/windows-live-messenger?os=other for more information.
7. Go to http://www.polycom.com/ for more information.
8. There is much useful material available that provides advice on holding teleconferencing meetings. I provide only the smallest bit of advice here. I recommend finding some of these resources and making sure your team is ready. Do not just pretend that a teleconferencing meeting is the same thing as a regular meeting; it is not, and you will be disappointed if you do not account for the differences in the meeting types.
9. As before, make sure that any whiteboard drawings and any flip chart pages are properly tagged with the ID of the backlog item being discussed.
10. When the team splits, you may want to keep everyone in the team room or conference room where the Sprint Planning meeting is being held. Letting people leave the vicinity often makes it more difficult to get them reengaged at the end of the time box.
11. As before, make sure that any whiteboard drawings and any flip chart pages are properly tagged with the ID of the backlog item being discussed.
12. As before, make sure that any whiteboard drawings and any flip chart pages are properly tagged with the ID of the backlog item being discussed.

6

The Daily Scrum Meeting

INTRODUCTION

The purpose of the Daily Scrum meeting is to give the Scrum team an opportunity as a team to "inspect and adapt" on a daily basis. When done properly, the Daily Scrum creates a clear picture of the team's current situation, allowing the team to make effective decisions about what to do next. In effect, the Daily Scrum provides the transparency and the opportunity to inspect its current situation, with adaptation coming right after the Daily Scrum meeting in the form of more discussion. And, of course, Scrum places great significance on "inspect-and-adapt"-type feedback loops to get the right things done at the right time.

PREPARING FOR THE DAILY SCRUM

There is no preparation necessary for the Daily Scrum except to make sure that everyone on the team understands how the Daily Scrum works and how to do it. When doing the Daily Scrum for the first time with a new team, you will probably want to schedule a little more time than normal to ensure that everyone is familiar with the rules for the meeting before you proceed (Figure 6.1).[1]

When scheduling the Daily Scrum, there is no rule on the right or wrong time of day during which to hold the meeting. In general, my advice is not to hold the meeting too early in the morning (before 10 a.m.) or too late in the afternoon (after 2:30 p.m.), as team members tend to require time to wake up in the morning and they often tend to begin mentally "shutting down" after 2:30 p.m. Whenever you and the

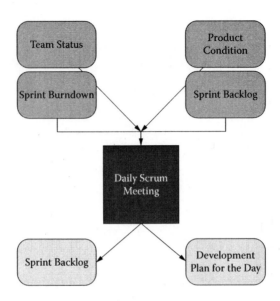

FIGURE 6.1
Inputs and outputs of the Daily Scrum meeting.

team decide to hold the Daily Scrum meeting, you should make sure of the following:

- Same time every day
- Same place every day, preferably near the team's task board (if applicable)
- Set aside 30 minutes for the Daily Scrum (15 minutes for the meeting and 15 minutes for the discussions that might follow)

Do not cancel the Daily Scrum for any reason[2] and make sure that the team understands that the absence of the ScrumMaster does not mean that the team should not do the Daily Scrum (after all, the meeting is for the team, not the ScrumMaster).

With geographically distributed teams, there are many versions of Daily Scrums that you can use and will be effective. We discuss setting up, facilitating, and wrapping up each type in the sections that follow.

THE STANDARD DAILY SCRUM (ALL TEAM MEMBERS IN ONE LOCATION)

Setup: There is really no setup required for this version of the Daily Scrum. Just get everyone together at the right time each day.

Facilitation: Once everyone has come together, or at the moment that the Daily Scrum is supposed to start, get everyone arranged in a semicircle facing the task board. Starting with the person to the left of the ScrumMaster, encourage everyone to answer the three Daily Scrum questions briefly, but with some detail. The three questions that need to be answered by each team member are

1. What have I accomplished since the previous Daily Scrum?
2. What do I plan to accomplish between now and the next Daily Scrum?
3. What, if anything, is keeping me from getting my work done?

After each team member answers the three questions, the team member to his or her left goes next. Once the last team member has answered the three questions, the meeting is over.

Once the Daily Scrum meeting begins, no one outside the team is allowed to ask questions or make comments. It is therefore helpful in some cases for the ScrumMaster to announce the beginning and the end of the Daily Scrum.

Wrap-up: Once the Daily Scrum meeting is over, you can invite comments or questions from people who may have attended the Daily Scrum but are not part of the Scrum team. This is also a good opportunity for people on the Scrum team to have conversations that might be necessary to decide what to do next based on what they heard or said during the Daily Scrum meeting.

There is absolutely no reason for the ScrumMaster or anyone else on the Scrum team to have a laptop or a notepad or to take minutes of any kind. Some team members might keep notes to remind them of whom they need to speak with after the Daily Scrum meeting is over. The ScrumMaster might keep notes to remind him or her of whom to followed up with after the Daily Scrum meeting in the case of impediments or obstacles.

THE TOKENIZED DAILY SCRUM (ALL TEAM MEMBERS IN ONE LOCATION)

Setup: This version of the Daily Scrum meeting requires a central table or area around which the team can gather. On that table, there is a token of some kind (a small stuffed animal, a ball, a trophy, a mug, etc.).

Facilitation: At the appropriate time, someone on the team (it does not need to be a designated person, just someone who has realized it is the right time to start the Daily Scrum meeting) yells something like, "Stand up!" or "Scrum!" It is on this signal that the entire team gathers around the prearranged central location, whether it is a table or the team's task board. In that prearranged location, the token is placed. Once the team gathers at the location for the Daily Scrum, the person standing closest to the location of the token picks up the token and answers the three questions mentioned in the previous section. When he or she is finished answering three questions, the token is passed (usually in the air) to the next nonadjacent person who has not yet answered the questions. It then becomes that person's turn to answer the three questions. The token is passed from team member to team member until everyone has had an opportunity to participate. Usually, the ScrumMaster and the Product Owner take part in answering the questions.

In some cases, teams have imposed minor penalties for passing the token to someone who has already answered the three questions (this is usually an amount as little as a quarter to as much as a dollar; when there is enough money collected, the team either spends it on food for the team or gives it to an agreed-on charity).

Wrap-up: As with the previous example, once the Daily Scrum meeting is over, you can invite comments or questions from people who may have attended the Daily Scrum but are not part of the Scrum team. This is also a good opportunity for people on the Scrum team to have conversations that might be necessary to decide what to do next based on what they heard or said during the Daily Scrum meeting.

As mentioned, there is no need for minutes to be taken during the Daily Scrum.

THE SLIGHTLY REMOTE DAILY SCRUM

Setup: This version of the Daily Scrum meeting is used when one or more of the team members is not colocated with the rest of the team. Therefore, at the location where the team holds the Daily Scrum meeting, there should be a speakerphone capable of clean and clear two-way communication between the team members and the member who is remote. Check your connection to the remote team member before the first Daily Scrum meeting.

It is best, for coordination purposes, to set up a teleconference phone line that can be used by the team every day for the Daily Scrum as well as other team meetings. This will become critical if there is more than one remote team member. If you have one or more remote team members, make sure you send teleconference phone line information with the invitation for the Daily Scrum.

Facilitation: Just before the beginning of the Daily Scrum meeting, you should either call the remote team member (if there is just one remote team member and you are using a single phone line) or you should call the teleconferencing line to ensure that a clean connection is available in order to hold the Daily Scrum meeting.

Once the Daily Scrum meeting begins, you can elect to hear from the remote team members either before all the local team members or after all the local team members have answered the three questions. Regardless of what order you handle the remote team members, everyone does the same thing—they answer the three questions clearly and briefly. Another variation on this method is to have each team member who answers the three questions decide who goes next. They can select someone at their location or select someone on the phone. As discussed in the previous Daily Scrum method, selecting a team member who has already answered the questions might subject one to a minor penalty.

Wrap-up: As with the previous examples, invite discussion or questions from others who attended the Daily Scrum but are not part of the team as well as discussions and questions between team members. Again, no minutes are taken.

THE COMPLETELY REMOTE DAILY SCRUM

Setup: This version of the Daily Scrum meeting is used when none of the team members is colocated. In other words, the entire team is remote. In this case, you will be using some form of teleconferencing into which all team members will dial each day to participate in the Daily Scrum meeting. When setting up this Daily Scrum, ensure that all team members have the phone line information and test their equipment to ensure that they can access the teleconferencing line before the first Daily Scrum meeting.

Facilitation: Just before the beginning of the Daily Scrum meeting each day, you should call the teleconferencing line to ensure that the meeting is ready to begin and that you have clean and clear access. At the point the Daily Scrum is about to begin, the rest of the team should dial in from their respective locations. It is important to ensure that all team members are aware of the starting time of the Daily Scrum meeting. Should you have difficulty getting your entire team on the teleconferencing line at the beginning of the Daily Scrum, be sure to follow up immediately to find out why people were late and what is needed to ensure that they are not late again.

In a case such as this, it is not uncommon for the ScrumMaster to start the meeting by answering the three questions him- or herself. He or she will then select the team member to go next (again, some teams impose a minor penalty when someone on the team chooses someone to go who has already answered the questions). Once everyone on the team has had an opportunity to talk, the meeting is over.

In this situation, team members will frequently continue to use the teleconferencing phone line to address information they want to discuss. If there are a number of conversations that need to occur, team members may often take this off line and establish conversations in other ways. However, it is not unusual for the team to decide to continue to use the teleconferencing phone line for up to 45 minutes after the Daily Scrum is ended to handle team business.

Wrap-up: The end of the Daily Scrum meeting is a good opportunity to allow others who may have attended the Daily Scrum but are not team members to ask questions of the team. As before, do not take minutes.

ENDNOTES

1. While the focus in Scrum is usually not on rules and prescriptive steps, it is important to manage the Daily Scrum with proper rules in place before you start. An ineffectively run Daily Scrum will almost always lead to ineffective decisions made as a result of the meeting.
2. The only time that the Daily Scrum does not occur is on the first and last days of the Sprint (when the Sprint Planning and Sprint Review/Sprint Retrospective meetings occur).

7

The Sprint Review Meeting

INTRODUCTION

The purpose of the Sprint Review meeting is to give the Scrum team an opportunity to review with the Product Owner what was completed during the previous Sprint to determine what to do next. As with the daily Scrum meeting, the Sprint Review meeting is part of Scrum's many "inspect-and-adapt" feedback loops. As such, the Sprint Review meeting is extremely important. Good facilitation is a key for holding an effective review (Figure 7.1).

PREPARING THE SPRINT REVIEW MEETING

The Sprint Review meeting happens the last day of every Sprint. It should be scheduled to take place usually during the morning or early afternoon of the last day, and invitations to the meeting should go to the team and other interested stakeholders at least several days in advance (since the sprint schedule is often known many months in advance, this should not pose a problem for the ScrumMaster). The location of the Sprint Review meeting is not terribly important; it works well in the team room (if one is available) or works equally well in a conference room. For the ScrumMaster, the important thing to keep in mind when planning the Sprint Review meeting is to keep the Scrum team focused on getting backlog items DONE so that there is something to review.

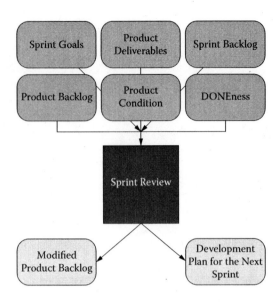

FIGURE 7.1
Inputs and outputs of the Sprint Review meeting.

SETTING UP THE SPRINT REVIEW MEETING

Setting up the Sprint Review meeting is a fairly straightforward process. There are, essentially, two activities that are going to occur during the meeting: demonstration and some "preplanning" for the next Sprint. So, you will want to go into the Sprint Review meeting with the following equipment:

- A data projector and projection screen
- A laptop or desktop that can access the integrated test environment from which the demonstration of completed functionality will be run
- A flip chart or whiteboard
- A digital camera
- Post-it notes, markers, whiteboard markers
- A list of the backlog items committed in the Sprint at Sprint Planning with an indication on each whether the team has called the backlog item DONE or not

Of course, the laptop/desktop and projector will handle the demonstration of the completed backlog items. But the flip chart, whiteboard,

Post-Its, and markers are important to facilitate any discussion of the backlog items, the Product Backlog, and the content of the next Sprint that might occur during the course of the Sprint Review meeting.

FACILITATING THE SPRINT REVIEW MEETING

Once the Sprint Review meeting begins, it is fairly free-form. You could try following these "rough" steps:

1. Each completed backlog item should be demonstrated to the Product Owner. The Product Owner may ask questions to gain a greater understanding. Team members may join the discussion or even ask more questions as the circumstances require.
2. The Product Owner decides whether or not the backlog item is DONE as demonstrated. There are a few potential outcomes for each demonstrated backlog item:
   a. The item is accepted by the Product Owner without changes. In this case, the ScrumMaster should mark the backlog item as "Accepted," and the item should be removed from the Product Backlog.
   b. The item is accepted by the Product Owner with some changes. In this case, the ScrumMaster should mark the backlog item as "Accepted," remove the item from the Product Backlog, *and* prompt the Product Owner to define, as one or more backlog items, the changes he or she would like placed in the Product Backlog.
   c. The item is not acceptable to the Product Owner. This may be because the item truly does not function as the Product Owner expected, or it may work perfectly but be in some violation of the organization's DONEness criteria. Typical DONEness failures include
      (1) Failure of a unit test or acceptance associated with the new or changed feature.
      (2) Failure of any kind of test resulting from integration of the new or changed feature.
      (3) Incomplete documentation or specifications.

      (4). Incomplete required process steps (e.g., an artifact or record that is supposed to be signed off, but is not).

3. Following the completion of the demonstration, conversation turns to what needs to be built during the next Sprint. While the Product Owner may have a specific idea of what he or she wants from each Sprint, the reality of what is finished and what is not usually causes some changes to those plans. For example, in one project, the Product Owner had a series of similar features that he wanted added to the product. He guessed that each feature would take about one Sprint to integrate properly into the product. The first Sprint ended with the first of the features mostly done but still missing some final steps. The Product Owner was not convinced that this would be a trend— "After all," he thought, "We were almost finished." Unfortunately, the performance of the team during the first Sprint was repeated in the second. At the second Sprint's Sprint Review meeting, it became obvious to the Product Owner that he had underestimated the effort involved with backlog items. At that point, he began revising both his short-term expectations (what is going into the next Sprint) as well as his longer-term expectations, resolving to speak with his customers early to explain that some of the desired features would not make it into the next Sprint.

How you facilitate the Sprint Review meeting, then, is a matter of personal preference. I encourage ScrumMasters to start the review by setting the stage—a quick recap of what was committed at Sprint Planning, followed by a quick review of which backlog items were completed and which were not. Some ScrumMasters go as far as opening the floor for discussion of why there were incomplete backlog items. I personally do not recommend discussing this here, as it can degrade into a finger-pointing session that, in the end, does not complete the demonstration of the product to the Product Owner before the team runs out of time. If you want to discuss why backlog items were not completed, discuss it at the Sprint Retrospective meeting.

I generally encourage ScrumMasters to let team members drive most of the Sprint Review meeting. Not only are they usually the most familiar with the functionality they will be demonstrating, but also it gives everyone on the team an opportunity to be noticed by other "higher-ups" in the organization.

Once the demonstrations are done and the decisions regarding the DONEness of backlog items are finished, the team should move into the discussion portion of the Sprint Review meeting. This, as with the rest of the meeting, is very free-form. As the goal of this portion of the meeting is to ensure that there is a go-forward direction for the next Sprint Planning meeting, you may need to facilitate this portion of the meeting as follows:

- Ask the Product Owner if he or she has any concerns regarding what was and was not finished during the Sprint with regard to the Product Backlog. Are there new items to be added?
- Ask the team if they have any concerns regarding the backlog items likely to be committed in the next Sprint. Since the team should have discussed the highest-priority backlog items during their backlog grooming workshops, they should have a good idea regarding what is coming up next. If something learned in the Sprint just ended raises concern about what is coming up next, this might be the right time to bring it up.

WRAPPING UP THE SPRINT REVIEW MEETING

The most important thing for the ScrumMaster to do by the end of the Sprint Review meeting (or very soon thereafter) is to ensure that the Product Backlog is properly updated with the results of the Sprint Review meeting.[1] Backlog items that were accepted by the Product Owner need to be updated and removed from the Product Backlog. New backlog items that resulted from the discussion during the meeting should be opened by the ScrumMaster and prioritized by the Product Owner as quickly as possible following the close of the Review meeting. Any backlog item not accepted by the Product Owner should be left in the Product Backlog *exactly as it exists at the end of the Sprint.* This means that any remaining, incomplete tasks need to remain with the backlog item to be carried into a future Sprint (do not forget to keep the tasks).

Note: When an "in progress" backlog item reaches the end of the Sprint still in progress, do not change its estimate to account for the remaining work. As you might know, Scrum teams do not get partial credit for work that is started but not finished during the Sprint. Likewise, the backlog item does not lose "size" just because it was started.[2] When the item is brought forward into a future Sprint, the team can assess how much work is actually left and make its total commitment considering the carried-forward backlog item. Let us look at an example:

> A Scrum team commits to 25 story points in Sprint 1. The last backlog item added to the Sprint during Sprint Planning had a size estimate of 3 story points. When the backlog item was solved and turned into tasks, the 30 tasks had a total size of 105 hours. At the end of Sprint 1, all backlog items except the aforementioned item were complete. Of that item, 50 hours of the tasks had been finished. The team finished the Sprint with an actual velocity of 22 story points.
>
> In the next Sprint, the team started with the 3-story-point backlog item from the previous Sprint. The team, looking at the remaining 55 hours from the previous Sprint, decided that they would commit to about 20 *new* story points, leaving some room for the old work. That gave them a total committed velocity of 23 (the new 20 points, plus the 3 points from the previous Sprint).

As a ScrumMaster, when you are done updating the Product Backlog from the results of the Sprint Review meeting, there should be *no* backlog items unaccounted for—every item originally committed to at Sprint Planning should either be closed and removed from the Product Backlog or left in the Product Backlog for a future Sprint.[3]

ENDNOTES

1. Scrum-aware tools, like VersionOne, ScrumWorks, and Rally, help the ScrumMaster and the Product Owner to keep the Product Backlog properly updated when a Sprint closes. At the time of this writing, other tools (like Microsoft TFS and JIRA/GreenHopper) were less aware of how Scrum works, putting more of the emphasis on the ScrumMaster to get it right. Look for more "out-of-sync" backlog items in these tools.

2. The fundamental concept here, while annoying to some, is sound. Business value is earned only when backlog items (which represent business value) are *completed*. There is no such thing as partial value. Either the value is in the product or it is not. Either the entire size of the backlog item is represented on the Product Backlog or it is not. You cannot have it both ways and maintain a clear measure of what is in the product and what is not.

3. Check your tool documentation, if applicable, for instructions on how to properly close out a Sprint.

8

The Sprint Retrospective Meeting

INTRODUCTION

The Sprint Retrospective meeting is held at the end of every Sprint, usually following the Sprint Review meeting. Where the purpose of the Sprint Review meeting is to review what the team built during the Sprint and what to do next, the purpose of the Sprint Retrospective meeting is to review how the team worked during the previous Sprint and to make improvements to its processes and practices (Figure 8.1).

Again, while the retrospective meetings are required as part of the Scrum framework, exactly how the meetings are run is up to you.

PREPARING FOR THE SPRINT RETROSPECTIVE MEETING

The length of the Sprint Retrospective meeting is not set. The meeting can be 30 minutes in length; it could be 2 hours and 30 minutes in length. For a new team, plan the meeting for 90 minutes and see what happens in that time period. Future retrospective meetings can be shorter or longer depending on how they work.

Retrospective meetings involve the entire team (including Product Owner and ScrumMaster). Where the meeting is held is not terribly important as long as it provides privacy for the team to encourage open dialogue.

I do not recommend inviting management to retrospective meetings or taking minutes of retrospective meetings. Both choices tend to limit the honesty and openness of the meeting. The only thing that anybody outside

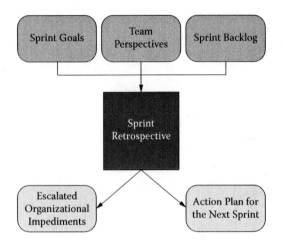

FIGURE 8.1
Inputs and outputs of the Sprint Retrospective meeting.

the team needs to know about what was discussed is what was decided ("the findings").

Another recommendation for Scrum teams is to make a team member responsible for the findings that arise from a retrospective. This responsibility, which would pass from team member to team member after each retrospective, would require the team member to ensure that the actions identified in the retrospective are carried out in the next Sprint. In addition, the team member would attempt to measure the success of the actions during the course of the Sprint (the measurement would not have to be formal or detailed; a simple observation that actions helped or did not help would be sufficient).

You should prepare an agenda before the Sprint Retrospective meeting. Because the meeting is all about discussion, exploration, innovation, and brainstorming, you need to time box every aspect of the meeting. This can help keep discussions short enough that the team gets something useful out of them while ensuring that the goals of the meeting can be accomplished without running out of time (or having an excessively long meeting). At a high level, you might want to start with something like the depiction in Figure 8.2.

Finally, it is a good idea to go into a Sprint Retrospective with an idea of the type of goal you want to achieve as the team's ScrumMaster—not that the ScrumMaster has any special authority, but the ScrumMaster approaches the Sprint much more attentively (looking at how everything is working together) than the typical team member, who is much more

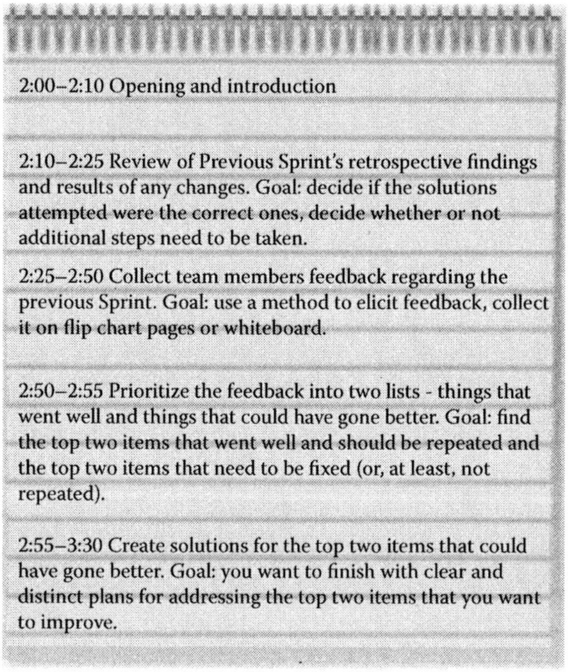

2:00–2:10 Opening and introduction

2:10–2:25 Review of Previous Sprint's retrospective findings and results of any changes. Goal: decide if the solutions attempted were the correct ones, decide whether or not additional steps need to be taken.

2:25–2:50 Collect team members feedback regarding the previous Sprint. Goal: use a method to elicit feedback, collect it on flip chart pages or whiteboard.

2:50–2:55 Prioritize the feedback into two lists - things that went well and things that could have gone better. Goal: find the top two items that went well and should be repeated and the top two items that need to be fixed (or, at least, not repeated).

2:55–3:30 Create solutions for the top two items that could have gone better. Goal: you want to finish with clear and distinct plans for addressing the top two items that you want to improve.

FIGURE 8.2
An agenda for a typical Sprint Retrospective meeting.

task and backlog item focused. Perhaps you want the team to focus on improved testing during the next Sprint, or maybe the team really needs to get better at getting to DONE on their backlog items. By going into the retrospective meeting with some goals of your own, you can help the team focus their feedback and their thoughts into areas that need improvement. Team discussion will often lead to other areas as well; this is to be expected. But, giving the team a place to start can be the difference between an effective retrospective and a meeting that produces many good thoughts but no real direction.

SETTING UP THE SPRINT RETROSPECTIVE MEETING

Setting up for the retrospective meeting is similar to setting up for any planning meeting. You will need most or all of the following materials:

- a conference room or the team room
- a central table
- flip charts or whiteboards
- a digital camera to capture work from whiteboards and flip charts
- Post-it notes, markers, whiteboard markers

To prepare the environment for the meeting, follow these steps:

1. Clear the table. Other materials on the table can be distracting.
2. Put the Post-its on the table with markers (make sure that the markers work).
3. Put the whiteboard markers with the whiteboard (make sure these markers also work).
4. Start the meeting on time.

FACILITATING THE SPRINT RETROSPECTIVE MEETING

When actually running the retrospective meeting, the easiest thing to do is to stick to the agenda you created before the meeting. Make sure everyone knows why they are there and what the goals of the meeting are and then follow your agenda.

- *Review items from the previous Sprint.* Item by item, the team reviews the results of the solution for the item in the previous Sprint. Was the solution effective? Did the solution solve the problem? Partially solve the problem? Create new problems? What are the next steps?
- *Collect the team's feedback from the current Sprint.* Through one of several different methods,[1] collect the team's feedback on what happened during the Sprint. Try to categorize into "things that went well" and "things that could be improved." Discuss all feedback, even if briefly, to ensure that everyone on the team understands what everyone else is trying to say. You may find, in fact, that you will need to spend more time on this activity than on anything else in the retrospective. Be prepared to rewrite your agenda based on your experiences from this meeting.
- *Prioritize each list.* This should never take more than a few minutes. There are a number of good methods for prioritization, including

a simple group vote that will solve this problem. For retrospectives done over the telephone (LiveMeeting, GotoMeeting, etc.), a simple polling function can provide a means to rapidly prioritize a short list of items. When everyone is together, you can simply put the lists on flip chart pages or a whiteboard and let the team vote. The method I use is to give everyone five or ten votes and let them spend their votes as they see fit, on one or more items.

- *Create solutions for the top two items that could be improved.* This is an important part of the retrospective meeting and the one most frequently mishandled. For the retrospective to have any positive value, the Scrum must create actionable steps to answer the top two items that could be improved. For example, I have worked with many new Scrum teams that have come out of a retrospective meeting with their number one could-be-improved item being, "Our Daily Scrums take too long." In many of these cases, the team finishes the Sprint Retrospective meeting recognizing the problem but saying nothing about a solution. In other cases, the team simply formalizes the lack of direction by saying something useless like, "We will hold shorter Daily Scrums" (this is not an action; it is, at best, a statement of intent). The proper answer for this kind of retrospective finding is to clearly identify *how* the team is going to shorten the Daily Scrums. In a few instances, the team has discussed the problem during the retrospective and decided to hold shorter Daily Scrums by giving everyone a time limit. In one specific instance, a team member stood during the Daily Scrum with an iPhone in his hand and a timer application running. The timer would make a noise at predefined times during the 2-minute slot that each team member was allocated to answer the three questions. The challenge was to use the signals to understand how much time the team member had to finish. After a few Sprints, each team member had learned what 2 minutes "felt like," and they were able to stop timing the meetings. They have never had a problem with the length of their Daily Scrums since then.

At this point, if all has gone well, your Sprint Retrospective meeting should be done, and you should have the following:

- one or two items that went well and the teams want to repeat

- one or two items that could have gone better along with specific steps that the team is going to take during the next Sprint to create the desired improvement

These are called the "retrospective findings."

WRAPPING UP THE SPRINT RETROSPECTIVE MEETING

If your team has decided to have someone on the team be responsible for the retrospective findings, great. If not, it will be your job—the ScrumMaster. Regardless of who does it, the job is to (a) post the retrospective findings where everyone on the team can see them and (b) work throughout the Sprint with the team to ensure that the steps that the team agreed to do get built into the Sprint Backlog and get done during the Sprint.

I would be unforgivably remiss if I did not make reference to Esther Derby and Diana Larsen's book on the Sprint Retrospective meeting called *Agile Retrospectives*. This is an excellent book and should be in the library of any serious ScrumMaster or agile coach. The book contains not only a simple process for handling retrospective meetings, but also a library of techniques for getting information out of a team and onto one form or another of paper. The various methods are well described and easy to put into practice.

ENDNOTE

1. For the best collection of retrospective methods, I recommend *Agile Retrospectives: Making Good Teams Great* by Esther Derby and Diana Larsen, Pragmatic Bookshelf, August 2006.

9

Creating Backlog Agreements

The creation of Backlog Agreements is a critical team responsibility that occurs during Sprint Planning and, sometimes, during the Sprint. I have had many Scrum teams do a Sprint Retrospective meeting and emerge with the number one item phrased something like this: "We need to understand backlog items better before tasking them out and committing to them."

Scrum team after Scrum team falls victim to the same trap. Many of us have grown so used to using written specifications to try to understand what we are going to build that we have lost our interrogative skills. Teams that clearly understand the acceptance criteria for their backlog items tend to do quite well during the Sprint. Other teams get lost, ask many questions, and experience many delays during the Sprint.

Creating a backlog agreement is all about understanding a backlog item so well that the team can create a solution for the item and then create all of the tasks necessary to create the solution (Figure 9.1). When I teach ScrumMasters and teams, I explain that, until Sprint Planning, we have deliberately avoided trying to understand how we are going to build something and have focused instead on what problem it is we are trying to solve. So, by the time we get to Sprint Planning, the team has done a pretty good job of understanding *what* the Product Owner wants us to build.[1]

When we create a backlog agreement at Sprint Planning, we are completely focused not on *what*, but on *how*.

The functional characteristics of a backlog item come in many different flavors. Here are some of the items you will want to consider when trying to fully understand a backlog item and some examples:

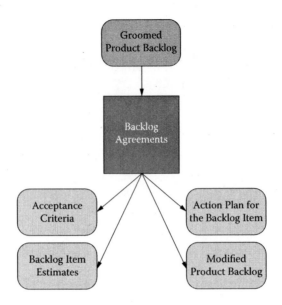

FIGURE 9.1
Inputs and outputs to create Backlog Agreements.

1. User interface (UI) considerations: What should the solution look like? It is not unusual for entire UI flows to be roughly documented on flip chart pages or whiteboard drawings during the Sprint Planning meeting. Some examples include
   a. The log-in screen will contain a field for a user name, a password, and a hyperlink to "remember me on this computer."
   b. The log-in screen also has a log-in button for when the user has provided both a user name and a password.
   c. The password will be a password-type input field.
2. Process flow: How should the function flow from one step to the next (or is the functional paradigm other than stepwise)? Examples include the following:
   a. If the user simply closes the log-in screen, the user is returned to the main page without the authority to do anything.
   b. If the user provides the wrong password three times, his or her account is locked, and a message is displayed on the log-in screen.
   c. If the user provides the right user ID and password, the user is allowed to sign on. The loading of authorizations is done later; for now, we return to the main page with the user name in the screen header (as per the UI standards).

3. Information display characteristics: How should the data be displayed? In what order? Can the user re-sort the display? Can the user change the display? Examples include the following:

   a. When the user lists the items in the store inventory, the list is provided in pages of 20 lines per page. Standard pagination controls (see the UI style guide) are used.

   b. The list is initially sorted by item inventory number. The user has the ability to change the sort order (ascending or descending) by clicking on the column header. Other columns that can be sorted in the same manner are item name, item price, and item quantity.

   c. The list includes the following items: item name, item inventory number, item quantity, item price, and item category (toys, electronics, food, men's clothing, etc.).

4. Security: What kind of authorizations are required for the function represented by the backlog item? Are there exceptions to the rule? Is there any kind of auditing done when the feature is used properly? What happens if someone attempts to use the feature without authorization? Examples include the following:

   a. The user must be signed on as an administrator before he or she can use this function.

   b. In case an unauthorized user gains access to the function, an additional check of the user's security tokens should be done before the function actually makes permanent changes to the database.

5. Performance: Are there performance characteristics for the backlog item? How fast does it have to be? Are there times when it can be slower? Examples include the following:

   a. The first page of the item inventory should display in less than 3 seconds from the moment that the user presses the "Display" button.

   b. Requests to page forward will be performed in less than 3 seconds.

In addition to the functional characteristics of the backlog item, the team might also discuss checkpoints or milestones in the development effort. For example, the Product Owner might require a wireframe of a user interface before the actual work is started.

Of course, there are many more possibilities for acceptance, limited only by the type of application you are building and the type of information needed to understand what needs to be built. It would be impractical and impossible to list all of the possible types of questions that may need to be answered to create acceptance criteria.

The key with acceptance criteria is to understand how much needs to be known to build what the Product Owner wants and when to recognize that sufficient acceptance criteria are at hand and that more information is not going to make the resulting feature better.

One practical technique I saw used with a Scrum team was the creation of a list of typical questions and topics that the Scrum team either asked frequently or forgot to ask during previous Sprints. During Sprint Planning, the ScrumMaster would copy a template of topics into the backlog item description (using a backlog management tool) as the team began to talk about each backlog item with the Product Owner. The ScrumMaster took notes, filling in areas of the template as appropriate and, when he thought necessary, would prompt the team to ask questions about areas on the template that were not getting filled in (note that the ScrumMaster did not ask the questions himself; he simply prompted the team to do so). Of course, this method takes a few Sprints to become effective, but it is a sound approach for teams that work on one product or similar products over a short period of time.

ENDNOTE

1. It is important, of course, to defer *how* we are going to build something until we have a good idea of *what* we are going to build. By doing so, we avoid a solution that does not solve the actual problem, and just as important, we have avoided wasting time trying to fathom out the technical solution until we are *very likely* to build the backlog item—at Sprint Planning.

10

Practical Advice to End the Practical Guide

Scrum is not a method. It is not a process. It is a framework made of practices and—most important–concepts. Most of this book is not about rules or "the only way to do things." This book and the advice in it are about practical answers to common problems. I do not expect that what you have read in the previous chapters and what you may read in the upcoming chapters will solve every problem that you experience. I do not expect that even the answers documented will perfectly and completely solve a particular problem you are having. What I do expect is that, as you read this book, you will begin to understand the concepts and principles on which Scrum and agile development have been created. Having gained that understanding, my hope is that the answers contained in this book will give you the clues that you need to solve the problems that you will experience.

Borrow entire answers, if you will, and use them. Use pieces of answers if it helps. Follow Scrum the way I have described it in the previous chapters, follow it the way you feel it should be done, or follow Scrum the way you were taught when you took the Certified ScrumMaster training. Alternatively, follow Scrum using all of these.

For myself, using agile development perfectly is not the point. Whether you subscribe to agile practices exactly as they have been documented in one "bible" or another, or whether you choose to use pieces of agile development that make sense for you to use—well, that is completely up to you. Use what works for you. In the end, the question you need ask is, "Is my customer more satisfied today than before?"

The bottom line in any software development effort is the satisfaction of the customer. Whether the customer is an astronaut depending on your software to bring him or her safely home or whether the customer is in another department in the same company where you work, the question is the same. If your customer is satisfied (or even happy) with what you are producing, then your software development efforts are working. To the extent that agile development has helped you improve your software quality and improve your customer's satisfaction, you can rest assured that you have used agile "correctly."

Section II

Questions Frequently Asked in CSM Training

11

About Agile Development

INTRODUCTION

I think it is safe to say that the term *agile development* will, in the long term, have more impact on software engineering than the terms *mainframe, client-server,* or *object-oriented programming.* The principles behind agile development suggest clearly that the more traditional approach to project, product, and people management may be fine for fields other than software development, but is not appropriate when we build software. For example, imagine building a house as an agile project. At the end of each 2-week iteration, the architect meets with the customer who says, "You know, it would be really cool if we could build a third floor." To which the architect answers, "Yes, it would, but the foundation was built to hold two floors; it might collapse under three floors." To add a third floor, the house would probably have to be torn down and rebuilt with a new foundation, costing the time and the materials.

Agile development focuses on the developers and the customers, bringing them closer together to build the right product. A second focus, on solid engineering practices, further helps us to build the product right through iterative product construction and continuous testing. A successful combination of good engineering practices and good collaboration practices gives us the right product right.

This chapter contains questions about agile development. What is it? How does it work? We start with one of the most fundamental questions about agile, concerning end dates.

DO AGILE PROJECTS HAVE END DATES?

On the surface, the quick answer here is—yes, of course agile projects have end dates—how else would you know you were finished? To satisfy one of the primary principles of agile development, the frequent delivery of valuable software, agile projects are organized around iterations that have concrete end dates. Therefore, at the end of the last iteration, the project is over.

There is more to this question, however, than just a query about a "never-ending" project. When one looks beneath the surface, the question is actually uncovering one of the most powerful aspects of agile development: Projects can be easily shortened or extended depending how good a job the organization does getting the valuable stuff done first while supporting the concept of DONEness within each iteration. To explain, let us first look at how a traditional waterfall project develops functionality. If one were to plot the amount of finished functionality over time in a waterfall project, the typical plot would look like the line graph in Figure 11.1.

As Figure 11.1 shows, completed functionality in a waterfall project occurs primarily in the latter half of the project. This is because the earliest stages of the traditional waterfall projects involve the creation of requirements-based documentation (market, program, or product requirement specifications) and functional design-based documentation (functional specifications, detailed design specifications, etc.) before the first line of code is written. So, while we can stop a waterfall-based project early, all we

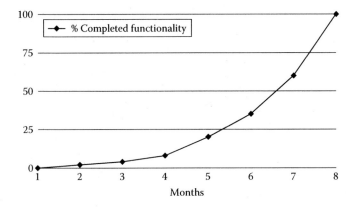

FIGURE 11.1
Approximation of features completed in a waterfall project.

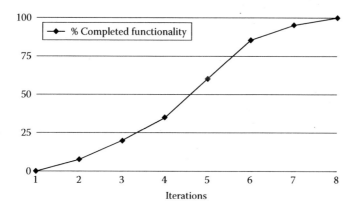

FIGURE 11.2
Approximation of features completed in an agile project.

will have to show for our efforts is a lot of documentation but little actual working functionality.

On the other hand, if we look at a project based on agile concepts we see a very different accumulation of completed functionality. Figure 11.2 shows a curve that represents the accumulation of completed functionality for a typical agile project. As each iteration of the agile project is executed, analysis, design, coding, and testing are all completed on many relatively small pieces of the overall functionality. In a waterfall project, that first month might have consisted almost completely of requirements analysis; the first iteration in an agile project consists of analysis, design, coding, and testing, and always results in parts of one or more features that we can show the customer. As a result, an agile project can be terminated early or extended easily and will always deliver some degree of functionality when ended. Because agile projects can be easily extended, it may seem like they do not end because you can just keep adding iterations.

However, personally, I do not recommend running a project longer than you need to, even if you have the option to add iterations. Users get impatient waiting for functionality, and their wants and desires change the longer you make them wait. Wait too long and, even though you will deliver what they asked for, they will not need it anymore. The old adage also works here: "Keep it short and simple."

WHAT IF MY CUSTOMERS DO NOT WANT EARLY AND FREQUENT DELIVERY?

Whenever I work with a customer who wants to transition their organization to agile development, there comes a point (usually early in the engagement) when the customer can be heard to say, "Wow! I had no idea that this would be this big!" This is usually right after the point when the organization management learns that doing agile development has an impact on your development organization, your customer service organization, and even your sales and marketing organization. Agile development also has an impact on your customers. For example, the first principle of Agile Development says that our "highest priority is to satisfy the customer through early and continuous delivery of valuable software." Well, what if your customer doesn't want your software "early and continuously?"

Let us take a simple case as an example: Jerry's Music Incorporated[1] is a growing sheet music and instrument sales company based in the Philadelphia area. Jerry's has been doing so well that its network of stores now spans 15 states and includes nearly 120 stores. The company formed an information technology (IT) group back in the mid-1980s; the IT group provides almost all of the software used by the stores and home office of the corporation. When the IT group started working, it ran their projects in a waterfall mode as mandated by their chief information officer (CIO), a 1975 graduate of Pennsylvania State University.[2] Software releases were rolled out on a somewhat regular basis, varying between 12 and 20 months. End users (the various internal departments and the stores) were usually happy with the results, but always unhappy with the wait.

In mid-2004, Jerry's Music's IT group switched to agile development (their CIO attended a session held by the Agile Philly users group in Philadelphia[3]). They rolled it out first in a pilot project (always a good idea) and then began doing more and more projects in an agile mode. In fact, they got so good at agile development they decided to announce that they would begin releasing new versions of the company's major software products every 6 months.

Expecting to be lauded as the new hero of the computer world, the CIO held a meeting with the home office department heads in the room and the regional office leadership on a conference line and a speakerphone. With a grand smile on his face, he announced the new release schedule. His smile disappeared when nearly every department head and every regional office leader started complaining, and even yelling, that he could not and should not go ahead with his plans.

It took a good 10 minutes to get everyone sitting and quiet again. For a short period, the conference phones were even muted just to give everyone a chance to catch a breath. With calm restored, the head of human resources (for no reason other than he was the only person who remained calm during the outbursts) asked one person to tell him why the CIO's plan was so unpopular. Others were also asked, and after a few minutes, the problem was clear: Whenever new software was released to the users, there was a resulting effort during which training, installation, and implementation was performed. There were even times when new hardware would have to be ordered. Since the 1980s, when the IT group started writing and releasing software, all departments that used the software had grown accustomed to not believing the release dates and delayed ordering new equipment or setting aside time for installation, implementation, and training until the IT group announced the third or fourth revised release date. "Even more important," the regional office leaders complained, "we have to test the new software every time there's a new delivery. When it was once a year or so, we didn't mind. But now you want to make it twice a year?"

There are many different types of users out there, and they each have their own unique needs. Users of Web sites, for example, have no problem with new features and new product versions every 60 days or so; I have worked with customers who updated their Web site every month. Others are fine with updates every 6 months (e.g., accounting or tax preparation software). But many end users want a product that works consistently, and as long as it does the job, they do not want it to require updates more frequently than once a year. As in the preceding example, some end users have to retest new versions of software. Many organizations have customizations of one kind or another in the product. Those customizations have to be retested every time a new version of code is installed. This could result in an extensive amount of work. That can leave your customers asking for less rather than more.

When you find yourself in this situation, my recommendation is to build small releases anyway. It is not necessary that every release be delivered to your customers. You could, for example, create a release every 6 months, completing new versions on March 1 and September 1. New customers would get the newest release available at the time of delivery; existing customers would get the September 1 releases only. The key is to keep your release timeframes long enough to create most major features from scratch while keeping the timeframes short enough that the release does not lose its focus (i.e., the overall goals of the release remain the same).

CAN YOU DO AGILE DEVELOPMENT WITHOUT SCRUM TEAMS?

You absolutely can do agile development without Scrum teams. Scrum is one of many development methods that fall under the "agile" umbrella, but the only one with Scrum teams. So, for example, you could go with Extreme Programming. You would still have teams, but no Sprints, no ScrumMaster, and no Scrum teams (you would have iterations and development teams instead). You could, for another example, use future-driven development FDD or Prince2, both of which use teams of developers, but not Scrum teams.

What it all boils down to is that agile development is *always* done with teams, not individuals. In fact, it is not just about any team of people. For a team to be truly agile, a number of things need to be true (no matter which agile method you use):

1. Skilled: For teams to be agile, they need to possess most, if not all, of the skills needed to get the job done that they are being asked to do. If they have to receive a partially complete work product from one group, do some tasks, and then pass the still-incomplete work off to another team, they cannot be very agile. Agile teams need to run with what they are building from beginning to end.

2. Collaborative: A hallmark property of agile teams is that they are collaborative. While this seems obvious, it is often a difficult state to attain. Developers used to taking their tasks, going to their desks, and typing away will find their working style radically changed. Agile teams work in groups, taking joint responsibility for multiple tasks and getting the work done together.

3. Self-organizing: Agile teams are not given preassigned tasks or predetermined solutions. Agile teams are given problems (e.g., user stories, backlog items) and are expected to determine a solution and organize themselves around the work.

4. Self-managing: Agile teams are generally expected to take on the responsibility for everything that needs to be done to properly build the product. Once the Product Owner has made it clear what the team is supposed to do, it is then up to the team to make it happen. Teams should correct the missteps and mistakes they make on their own (or get help to have necessary changes made to the organization) without being instructed to do so.

In short, while you can definitely use agile development without Scrum teams, you cannot use agile development without teams.

WHAT IS THE DIFFERENCE BETWEEN AGILE AND SCRUM?

Agile and Scrum are two different, but related, things. Let us look at this from a couple of different perspectives, starting with the historical.

The story here is an interesting one, as most of the methods we now associate with agile development actually existed before the term "agile development was coined. Essentially, Scrum was defined during the late 1980s and through the 1990s by the efforts of Ken Schwaber and Jeff Sutherland. Similarly, Dynamic Systems Development Method (DSDM), Feature-Driven Development (FDD), and Extreme Programming (XP) all existed to one degree or another prior to the coining of the phrase. In 2001, the leading experts for each of the existing methods (and others that were "very" involved) came together to create some clarity and consistency across the many methods that existed, culling from them the fundamental premises on which the methods were based. The result was called agile development. So, rather than being the same thing, Scrum actually pre-dates the agile moniker.

At the same time, it is not unusual that one might look at Scrum and Agile as the same thing. Scrum has been *very* popular since its introduction to the general population in 2002 and is the most used of the agile methods. I am not suggesting that Scrum is somehow better than the other methods—it is simply more popular.

What also sets Scrum apart from the rest of the agile methods is that it is also the only agile method that focuses solely on the "people" side of product development, rather than both the people and the technical sides.

Scrum is frequently used by groups that do not even build software. I have experience with management teams using Scrum as a way to coordinate activities. I have worked with human resources teams that use Scrum to prioritize their work and coordinate their efforts.

Most important, you should be aware that, in a software development environment, Scrum by itself is not enough. In other words, not only are Scrum and agile development two different things, but Scrum is not generally enough if you really want to do agile development. Scrum does an excellent job of defining how the team should work and how the team decides what they are going to build. But Scrum does not attempt to tell you how to build software. If you want to write software in an agile manner, you will want to employ some of the practices made popular by XP, like continuous integration and continuous testing.

So, Scrum and agile development are two different, but related, things. But if you want to do agile development well, I would recommend using Scrum as a starting point and add XP software engineering practices to really see results.

WHAT IS THE DIFFERENCE BETWEEN A USER STORY AND A USE CASE?

For the question of the difference between them, we should begin by defining both a user story and a use case. They are two very different constructs used for requirements analysis. The *user story* finds its roots in agile development (XP to be precise) and is defined as a reminder to have a conversation with the customer about something the customer wants "done" to the product. The user story, then, describes anything from a very large change that the customer wants all the way down to a very small incremental change to the product—all seen as valuable to the customer. Perhaps the best practical definition of user stories that I have found is the following:

> User stories are one of the primary development artifacts for Scrum and Extreme Programming (XP) project teams. A user story is a very high-level definition of a requirement, containing just enough information so that the developers can produce a reasonable estimate of the effort to implement it. ("Introduction to user stories," 2009)

> "I want to play chess on my notepad computer."

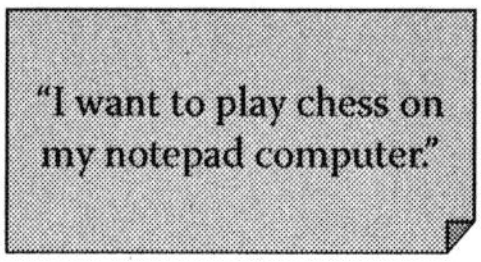

FIGURE 11.3
A rather large user story.

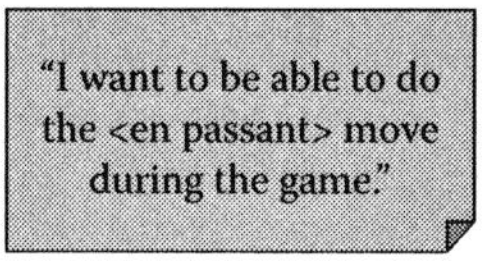

> "I want to be able to do the <en passant> move during the game."

FIGURE 11.4
A rather small user story.

On the other hand, Kurt Bittner and Ian Spence (2002) defined a *use case* as follows:

> Use cases represent the things of value that the system performs for its actors. Use cases are not functions or features, and they cannot be decomposed. Use cases have a name and a brief description. They also have detailed descriptions that are essentially stories about how the actors use the system to do something they consider important, and what the system does to satisfy these needs. (pp. 3–4)

Ironically, I do not believe that the authors were referring to user stories when they claimed that "they also have detailed descriptions that are essentially stories," but in reality these descriptions are often on target. You see, user stories can be of any size. They can describe relatively large pieces of functionality (Figure 11.3). The user story in Figure 11.3 potentially describes a whole new chess application for a notepad computer. It is a user story simply because it describes the desired functionality from the standpoint of the customer.

I could also have a user story like that in Figure 11.4. This user story describes a much smaller piece of functionality (a specific type of move available only under certain conditions) as opposed to describing an entire game, as the previous story example did.

Use cases usually describe larger pieces of functionality (much like the first user story) while also containing smaller scenarios that describe smaller, more specific pieces of functionality (like the second user story). To that degree, perhaps, user stories and use cases are similar. The true and critical difference between user stories and use cases has nothing to do, however, with their size or how they are written.

Scrum and XP both incorporate a principle of lean software development that essentially "defers decisions until the last reasonable moment" (more on this in Chapter 4). By deferring until the last reasonable moment, we ensure that we make decisions based on the reality of the current situation, with all of the available information, rather than attempting to guess the right decision too early. User stories support this concept, while use cases, generally, do not.[4] User stories are, when written, deliberately short on detail.

IS TIME FOR RESEARCH PART OF THE ITERATION?

Whether there is time allocated in an iteration for research depends primarily on the reason for the research and the value brought by doing it. Essentially, we create time in the iteration for research in one of two methods. First (and more commonly), we can create research time simply by creating backlog items (often called "analysis stories" or "spikes") that are committed to an iteration and, thus, completed during the iteration.

The second method for including time for research in the iteration is simply to allocate more time for research to an existing backlog item. Tasks to support the research are created during iteration planning and performed during the iteration.

The third method for doing research is for the research to be done by the Product Owner (without using any other team resources). In this instance, the work done outside the iteration is not technically part of the iteration.

In general, however, research is performed only if the Product Owner, customer, or development team cannot answer one or more questions about a backlog item and, without the information, cannot properly build the backlog item.

For example, imagine that a Product Owner or customer asked their development team to build a feature that was to process a billion transactions per day. The customer asked how this feature would perform and if it were actually possible to build. Unfortunately, the development team does not know if it is possible to process that many transactions and does not feel comfortable committing to a billion transactions per day. To answer

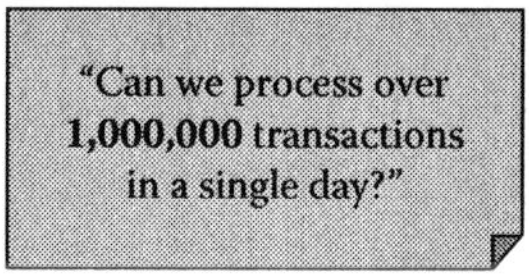

> "Can we process over
> **1,000,000** transactions
> in a single day?"

FIGURE 11.5
An analysis story.

the Product Owner's question, the team recommends an analysis story be added to the Product Backlog. The analysis should be phrased in such a way that answers the Product Owner's question. Therefore, we may create a new backlog item (Figure 11.5).

We will also, rather than determining the complexity or "size" of the item, simply limit the duration of the backlog item to an amount of time deemed by the team to be adequate to get the work done. In other words, instead of giving the backlog item a size of 34 story points, our research item might be given a 2-day time box. This practice helps us to ensure that research stories do not gain a life of their own, costing the organization more than necessary and yielding poor results, too many results, or no results.

So yes, to the extent that research yields information important to the development of the product, research is, in fact, included in the iteration time box when the research is done by the team.

WHAT HAPPENS IF WE DISCOVER SOMETHING WE SHOULD HAVE DONE DIFFERENTLY?

It happens all the time in software development—we make a design decision today that ends up being the wrong decision 4 or 5 months from now. In this situation, we are said to have encountered a "blocker." Our database design will not work the way we need it to; an application feature cannot support new and previously unexpected functionality. No matter which development method you use, one of these days it will happen to you. The question, however, assumes that we would catch these problems in waterfall development, where the analysis and design is completed up front, while in agile development we are exposed because we do the analysis and design as we go. Fortunately for agile development, that premise is, for the most part, wrong. Sure, there are outlying circumstances for which up-front analysis and design will catch blockers early. However, in most cases, blockers are subtle and none too easy to find, whether you do all of your analysis and design up front or you do your work progressively, as in agile development. They usually appear during the code-writing and -testing activities when the developer discovers an inability to continue as a result.

Agile development does have one advantage over waterfall, however. Because agile development builds working functionality as we go, blockers are found much sooner and can often be fixed with much less effort than when discovered in waterfall development methods.

In many agile projects, we attempt to mitigate these types of problems in three ways. First, it is advisable to complete an architecture review and to update your architecture definition before beginning feature development of a new or existing product. By doing so, you are more likely to identify potential blockers and less likely to run into problems during feature development (when application developers need to understand where the architecture "ends" and where the application features "begin"). Second, it is often a good idea to front-load risk—that is, to identify some of the riskiest backlog items in the project and build those items first. This way, should your teams discover a blocker (or a substantial risk for a blocker), they can take steps early, before a significant amount of new code is written. Third, it is *always* advisable to continuously refactor your code as you write it. Refactoring helps keep your code simple and structured, reducing the possibility of blockers occurring and, when they do, making the overall solution easier to implement.

But, if the worst happens, and the blocker does indeed strike despite all of our best efforts, your best options are to do the following:

1. React immediately. Do not wait until later to implement a solution because you have a delivery date to keep. Delaying the solution will only result in increasing problems down the line, coupled with increasingly expensive solutions. In all likelihood, addressing the problem immediately is your best bet for achieving your feature requirements in the least amount of time.

2. Solve the problem in front of you. Just because you are blocked does not mean that you want to solve this particular problem now and forever. In other words, let us say you have discovered that an application that needs to support 100 users can only reliably support 25. This is not the time to try to support 500 users just because you do not ever want to have to solve this problem again. By doing so, you

are only making the problem worse than it is and quite likely making the product much more expensive and difficult to configure than it actually needs to be.

HOW DO I COMMUNICATE EXPECTATIONS BEYOND THE PRODUCT OWNER?

There are a number of different ways of looking at the question of how you communicate expectations beyond the Product Owner. Each perspective is based on a different type of relationship with the customer. For example, if my customer tends to be very involved with the development effort and helpful when it comes do prioritizing and trimming the "want to haves" from the "must haves," my approach will probably be to provide full exposure to what is going on in the project in terms of the state of the release backlog and the future predictions made by using release backlog item size and team velocities. This means that my customer will have a fairly complete representation of the release backlog along with projections of what will be completed by the end of the current Sprint, by the end of the next Sprint, by the end of the Sprint after that, and so on.

Can that kind of exposure cause problems? Definitely. You probably will not provide that much detail to a customer unless you are (a) contractually obligated, (b) working closely with the customer and need that kind of communication, or (c) want to have to explain every prioritization, staffing, and technical decision made during the project that does not obviously improve velocity and how much feature/function the customer gets.

Regardless, if you are doing agile development, one thing is certain: You are going to communicate with your customers a lot more than you did before. You need only look at the principles on which all agile methods are based to see the truth, and inevitability, in the first of the principles:

Our highest priority is to satisfy the customer through early and continuous delivery of valuable software. This is the first, and arguably most important, of the 12 principles. Its very wording absolutely requires a great deal of customer interaction. "To satisfy the customer" requires that we understand which conditions satisfy the customer, and further, that we are continuously verifying our customer's satisfaction.

For the most part, what you want to communicate to your customers are the following points:

1. If the price or time is fixed, your customer needs to understand that you can make considerable changes in scope or content as they see fit, but everything comes at a price. If something new is added to the project content, something else will have to come out. I look at it like a 5-gallon bucket (or a 20-liter bucket, if you prefer) filled with water. When we start the project, the bucket is full. If we want to add more scope to the project (more water to the bucket), something (of equal size or larger) has to come out first (or it just ends up all over the floor).
2. Progress is measured by determining the approximate amount of work done each iteration and projecting that same progress against the remainder of the work. How much work our development teams can do during an iteration is called the *velocity*. Velocity is *not* constant; it changes a little every iteration, making our predictions just that—predictions.
3. Work is done in priority order; getting the greatest value done as early as possible. The hope is that any work dropped off the bottom of the list will be the least important and the easiest to remove from the project without losing significant functional value.

REFERENCES

Introduction to User Stories. 2009. *Agile Modeling*. http://www.agilemodeling.com/arti-facts/userStory.htm
Bittner, Kurt, and Ian Spence. 2002. *Use Case Modeling* New York: Addison-Wesley.

ENDNOTES

1. Jerry's Music Incorporated is a completely fictional company. While there are companies similar to it, I chose a music and instrument sales company simply because I am a closet percussionist and need an outlet.
2. Yep, I am still making this up. I am hoping my editor will ask me to write a new fictional series of books based on a music store in Hoboken, New Jersey.
3. You can find links to Agile Philly on my Web site, http://www.artisansoftwareconsulting.com/agilephilly
4. It is possible to write use cases in progressive mode, like user stories, but this generally is not done.

12

About Scrum

INTRODUCTION

As agile methods go, Scrum is unusual. It deliberately challenges the individual and the organization to become disciplined in their approach to software development. It is deliberately nonprescriptive, making it easy to understand its framework while simultaneously demanding a great deal of focus and involvement if you take it on. It does not talk about writing software, because the people who put the framework together knew that if you were to get your people working together first, those people would organize the best development practices for them and make it work because they were empowered to make those decisions. Even well-known and experienced agilists still draw comparisons between Scrum teams and XP teams, saying that XP teams are better because Scrum does not provide the development structure necessary to create and maintain high-quality code and XP does. Scrum, when properly taught, emphasizes the fact that a solid engineering infrastructure and solid engineering practices are required to get a good result. More importantly, Scrum emphasizes the "people" aspect of software development. That might explain why there are so many more Scrum teams in the world than XP teams. Regardless, when I coach an organization in the implementation of Scrum, I also discuss with the organization its testing and integration practices. I always implement Scrum as a team and work management framework using XP practices like test-driven development, continuous integration, continuous testing, pair programming, collective code ownership, customers on the team, user stories, and so on as a means of creating the solid engineering practices and infrastructure that are necessary.

This chapter talks more about Scrum and answers common questions about when Scrum should be used and what options you have to solve certain predictable problems.

IS SCRUM OF VALUE WITH PURE INFRASTRUCTURE OR COMMERCIAL, OFF-THE-SHELF (COTS) SOFTWARE PROJECTS?

Absolutely—Scrum is of value when developing applications as well as when implementing commercial, off-the-shelf (COTS) products. Scrum is not about writing software (even though that is the environment in which it grew up). In fact, Scrum is frequently used in nonsoftware development environments. Scrum is about teams collaborating to get the right things done in the right order. The Product Owner defines the right order and "what" the right things consist of. The team decides how things will get built (or get done). For infrastructure and commercial-off-the-shelf projects, just because the team is not writing software does not mean that the same principles cannot apply. For example, let us look at some of the potential backlog items we might have on our backlog were we to be planning an implementation of a new, off-the-shelf general ledger (GL) system:

- A chief financial officer (CFO) might want to evaluate up to three leading GL products to determine which one best meets the specific requirements of his or her company. Acceptance criteria added later to the backlog item would elaborate on the CFO's "specific requirements" and other needs and constraints.
- Implement and pilot the GL system for specific accounts and across one or two end-user groups. As we spoke more with the CFO and other accounting types, we would likely clarify the accounts and groups to be piloted.
- Extend the pilot across the organization, providing all necessary training and support. This backlog item would probably slice into all sorts of items, adding new end-user groups, creating tip sheets and instructional training, building and training support teams, and so on.

So, when we start looking at the Scrum teams we might need, we would again stick to the fundamental requirements of a Scrum team. Specifically, that the team is

1. Between five and nine individuals in size
2. Cross functional
3. Self-managing

Assuming a simple situation of only a single team, let us staff this team with

1. Two accountants from the accounting group; they would need specialization in GL products and how the company wants to use the new GL system.
2. A technical writer to help guide the creation of documentation about the new GL product and how it is used in the organization.
3. An information technologist to help ensure that all steps related to information technology (IT) (acquiring and setting up hardware and software, creating user IDs, and providing proper security and access) are handled in a timely basis.
4. A tester to help guide the creating of test procedures that ensure that the GL system is functioning properly.
5. A programmer to help with scripts or custom programming necessary to get the GL system working properly.
6. A process manager to help create proper process and procedure documentation that ensure that the system is used properly once training is provided.
7. An education specialist to help create and update the training materials as the project progresses.

This leads us to a quick look at what might be accomplished during the first couple of Sprints.

Sprint 1: Following a kickoff led by the CFO, the team's accountants help to identify the GL products that require evaluation. The entire team works together to determine evaluation criteria that include the CFO's criteria as well as look at

- ease of use
- minimum hardware and software configuration

- available training materials
- ease of customization
- testability

Not surprisingly, the team's evaluation criteria (beyond those provided by the CFO) are closely aligned with the team's various skills and areas of expertise. Already, our cross-functional team is paying off; we are looking at GL software packages with a much broader view than previous efforts might have included.

The Sprint continues with the team evaluating each of the candidate GL systems.

The Sprint ends with an evaluation of each product based on the internal requirements, as well as the scheduling of on-site demonstrations of the products by each of the product vendors during the timeframe of the second Sprint.

Sprint 2: This sprint begins with an on-site demonstration of the first GL product, which is attended by the team, the CFO, and a few other stakeholders. A demonstration version of the product is made available to the team by the vendor, and the team spends a few days doing a hands-on evaluation of the product. The other two candidate products are likewise demonstrated and evaluated by the team. By the end of the Sprint, a recommendation is made to the CFO with regard to which product to purchase. A decision is expected during the timeframe of the third Sprint.

Sprint 3: While the CFO's decision is pending, the team begins creating a rollout plan (which will not significantly vary regardless of which product is chosen). The fundamentals of the plan are that a small number of pilot teams will be selected. During this period, formal training, formal support plans, formal process and procedure documentation, product customizations, and automated tests will be drafted and revised. Once the pilot groups are successfully completed, a general and complete rollout will be started. Sprint 3 ends with the final decision by the CFO to choose one of the candidate products. The team starts the process of acquiring and installing the software.

Sprint 4: The GL software is installed and verified. Minor company-specific customizations are completed. Automated tests are planned and written. The accounting personnel on the team help determine naming conventions and other configuration settings.

Initial pilot team training and supporting documentation are created.

Sprint 5: The first pilot team is trained. Documentation is provided to support the training. A team member is always present to answer questions and collect feedback. The team routinely reviews the feedback to either improve the implementation or update the training materials.

As you can see in this example, although we discussed several Sprints, little to no coding or product development has taken place. If there is work to do, we can use the concepts and principles of Scrum to organize the work and make sure that it gets done in an effective manner.

WHEN IS SCRUM NOT A GOOD METHODOLOGY TO USE?

I have not yet found a project that would not benefit from the collaboration, value focus, and customer orientation brought to projects by methods like Scrum. However, technically, there are projects for which the benefits of Scrum are not realized nearly as much as in others.

Fundamentally, products (like many other systems) fall into one of four realms of "hardness" based on how well we understand the technology employed by the product and how well we understand the requirements of the product. Products can be

- Simple: Both the technology and the requirements are clearly understood.
- Complicated: Either the technology or the requirements are less-than-clearly understood.
- Complex: Either the technology or the requirements are not understood (or both are not clearly understood).
- Anarchic: Neither the technology *nor* the requirements are understood.

The benefits of Scrum are more obviously realized when developing a product that is either complicated (difficult to understand) or complex (large and difficult to predict). There are no methods I am aware of that function well in the anarchic space.

For products that are simple (easy to understand and predict), Scrum works, but many other methods (including waterfall) would work just as effectively. When the technology is clear and the requirements do not change, developers can estimate and predict with improved effectiveness, and there is considerably less likelihood of rework resulting from making design decisions earlier than necessary.

To put it more succinctly, waterfall processes work fine when working on a project for which the requirements change *extremely* little (bordering on "not at all") and the technology is *completely* understood and very unlikely to cause any unexpected difficulties. In my years working as an IT professional, I have run across only a few instances of projects that meet the criteria of no requirements change and completely understood technology. One good example I can use for which waterfall worked nearly as well as Scrum is in the case of a team that reported to me, their manager, several years ago.

This team of eight was responsible for building transaction-based interfaces between the various products that communicated with "our" product. The number of interfaces was substantial: There were at least 25 different types of interfaces and at least 20 vendors for each type of interface, so we had a library of well over 400 interfaces. Now, these interfaces were pretty much all driven by tools in our product, and most of them followed a popular "standardized" protocol that all of the vendors in the marketplace were beginning to support. In fact, because of the tools and the standardization, building interfaces quickly became a matter of agreeing on which events and which transaction segments were to be supported (data elements themselves became less and less of a problem; if a vendor did not support a data element, the vendor simply ignored it). This team's projects, building interfaces, became a matter of understanding how the vendor supported the standard protocol and then making (usually) minor modifications to create the interface. In other words, the requirements (the interface structure) became known, and the tools became predictable. For this team at that time, waterfall would have worked just as well as Scrum because everything the team did was a known and predictable activity—few surprises occurred during interface development.

DOES THE PRODUCT BACKLOG CONTAIN ALL REQUIREMENTS/STORIES?

The *Product Backlog* is defined as an ordered list of items that identify valuable work to be done to the product. We put our features here, our defects here (sometimes), and all of the rest of the work that we need to do to build the product (test environment setups, analysis stories, third-party package upgrades, product-specific training, etc.). To that end, the Product Backlog is the root of all of the work that we do. But, even within this definition of the Product Backlog, we recognize that not everything is known about a given item until after the Scrum team has actually built the item. In other words, we learn more and more about the items on the Product Backlog, up to and during Sprint Planning and even during the Sprint when the item in question is under construction.

The fact that the content of the Product Backlog cannot be accurately understood until after construction begins affirms the emergent nature of the Product Backlog as well as the concepts set forth in the "uncertainty principle of software development": The requirements of an application cannot ever be completely known until it is built (Schiel 2010, 299–301).

So, the Product Backlog is, in fact, the root source of *all* work to be done on a product and thus the root source of all requirements that are eventually identified during construction. However, the Product Backlog may not, in and of itself, identify or embody all of those requirements at the beginning of the project simply because many of the requirements not initially known are identified during Sprint Planning and during the Sprint.

DOES USING SCRUM MEAN THERE IS NO REASON FOR MANAGEMENT?

I think the short answer to the question of whether using Scrum means there is no reason for management is an emphatic "No!" Given the primary functions of management—staffing, budgeting, controlling—one need only look at the Scrum framework to see that none of those functions appears in Scrum. Without management, there would be no one to handle the bringing on of new employees. Even if the team plays a significant role in interviewing and approving candidates, it makes no sense for the Scrum team to handle the follow-up work that is necessary to do once a new employee is hired. When an employee does not perform well on one Scrum team, who is going to evaluate the situation to see if, perhaps, the employee might work better on a different team or should simply be discharged? The Scrum team? I am pretty sure that would constitute a conflict of interest.

More important, management plays a significant role in supporting Scrum teams by helping remove obstacles, by communicating business strategies and policies to the employee population in a consistent manner, by providing a "bigger picture" perspective for employees, by helping individual employees improve their skill set or resolve personal problems, and simply by handling all of the day-to-day administration that keeps the business going. Like the ScrumMaster, nearly everything the manager does is geared toward keeping the Scrum teams highly focused and highly productive.

At the same time, no discussion of this topic would be complete without talking about the role of management with regard to a Scrum team. While I explored this topic more fully in *Enterprise-Scale Agile Software Development* (Schiel 2010, 299–301), it is important to review the impact that a manager can have on a Scrum team. When providing support to a Scrum team (removing obstacles, resolving conflict, providing administrative assistance), a manager can be a positive influence on the proper functioning of the team. On the other hand, when a manager gets involved in the daily discussion and decision making of the team, he or she can inadvertently sap the self-managing function of the team. As a manager, one continuously walks a thin line between trying to provide support to the team and trying to avoid having the team (willingly or unwillingly) turn over their empowerment.

Here is a list of dos and don'ts that managers can apply to help them properly work with Scrum teams:

- *Do* ensure that Scrum teams know what they are building and why. If they do not have a clear understanding, ask the Product Owner to fill them in.
- *Do* respect the Scrum process. Do not schedule meetings when the team is supposed to be doing Sprint Planning, Daily Scrums, Sprint Reviews, or Sprint Retrospective meetings.
- *Do* come into the office on time each morning and leave on time in the afternoon. Do not expect your employees to work a full day if they think you do not.

- *Do* discourage gossip and rumors. They waste time and distract employees from getting work done.
- *Do* set high standards for your behavior toward employees and hold to those standards at all times.
- *Do* ensure that teams have the training they need to get the job done.
- *Do* ensure that *you* have the training you need to get the job done.
- *Do* build rapport with teams through honesty and professionalism.
- *Do* help teams understand the nature of the commitment they make at Sprint Planning. Say things like, "Do you truly believe you can finish this, at a high level of quality, by the end of the iteration?" "Do you really feel committed?"
- *Do* encourage others to admit their part in mistakes and allow them to learn from those mistakes.
- *Do* steer teams in the right direction if you feel they have missed an important element in their solution.
- *Do* support individuals who do not seem to understand agile practices or teamwork. Coach them toward better performance but always be prepared to look for better options for the individual.
- *Do* support the team when they ask for help.
- *Do* coach teams to improve their performance.
- *Do* coach teams to efficiently make sound decisions.
- *Don't* keep secrets from your staff. They know when you are doing it, and they probably know what it is you are not telling them.
- *Don't* try to win them over by sharing your weaknesses and fears.
- *Don't* worry about undercommitment. If the team can do more, they have a backlog of items they can go to for more work.
- *Don't* blame others for your mistakes. Take responsibility for your part in mistakes.
- *Don't* teach. You can lead, share, encourage, and stimulate team members to grow, develop, and learn.
- *Don't* take responsibility for your team's commitment.
- *Don't* make decisions for the team.
- *Don't* solve the team's problems for them; that is what you hired *them* to do.
- *Don't* take over if your team makes a mistake; encourage them to understand what they did wrong and to find a way to do it more effectively.

- *Don't* participate in Daily Scrums. You have to wait your turn until after the Daily Scrum is over, just like everyone else who is not on the Scrum team.

WHAT ARE THE DIFFERENCES BETWEEN SCRUM AND XP?

The term *agile development* is actually an umbrella term for several methods that share similar fundamental principles. Scrum and XP are both agile development methods. They share a lot of similarities because they are both agile methods, but they also have a lot of differences. Let us look at some of the similarities:

1. Both Scrum and XP are iterative. This means that they both work in terms of time boxes called iterations. Product is created in small slices by the end of each iteration. In XP, iterations are usually 1 or 2 weeks long. In Scrum, iterations are called Sprints and are usually 1, 2, 3, or 4 weeks long or 1 calendar month in length.

2. In XP, iterations begin with a Planning Game, in which the intended content of the iteration is planned out in detail in terms of user stories and tasks on a storyboard. In Scrum, iterations (Sprints) begin with a Sprint Planning meeting at which the intended content is planned out in detail and listed as a series of tasks on a list called a Sprint Backlog. For the most part, there is little difference between XP's storyboard and Scrum's Sprint Backlog, which is frequently represented and managed by some Scrum teams as a storyboard.

3. During an iteration, XP teams work collaboratively with their customers, building and reviewing continuously. Daily planning occurs at the team's daily stand-up meeting. During a Sprint, Scrum teams work collaboratively with their customers, building and reviewing continuously. Daily planning occurs during and immediately after the team's Daily Scrum meeting.

4. At the end of the iteration, XP teams deliver working functionality. What *deliver* means, however, can be broadly defined. Deliver can literally mean delivery to a production environment (like a Web site). Deliver can also simply mean adding new functionality to the "shelf," building a new release of software from the output of several

iterations. Similarly, Scrum teams end their Sprint with a Sprint Review meeting at which the completed functionality is reviewed. As with XP, sometimes the completed functionality is immediately released; sometimes it is collected with other functionality and released collectively.

5. After the end of the iteration, XP teams are encouraged to review their performance (called a "retrospective") to raise awareness of the team's strengths and abilities as well as where they can improve their performance. The team is expected to identify specific steps they can take to improve their performance and to carry those steps into the next iteration. Likewise, Scrum teams perform a Sprint Retrospective following the Sprint Review meeting. Some teams actually perform the Sprint Retrospective before the Sprint Review, and others wait until after Sprint Planning for the next Sprint; in nearly all cases, it is not advisable to hold the Sprint Retrospective meeting at any time other than shortly *after* the Sprint Review meeting.

6. In both XP and Scrum, teams are built with the necessary skills to get the job done. They are encouraged to work collaboratively and in a colocated space (although this is not a requirement). Teams organize themselves around their work, deciding, without a controlling focus (manager), what manner of solution they will employ and how they will implement their solution.

Now, let us look at some of the ways in which Scrum and XP differ:

1. XP is very much about software engineering. With practices like test-driven development (TDD), collective code ownership, and continuous integration, XP was created to bring agile development directly to the development team. Even the name, Extreme Programming, clearly spells out the focus of the method ("programming"). Although it grew up in software development environments, Scrum is actually more about people, saying nothing specific about software engineering in any aspects of the framework. While XP talks about both team behaviors and software engineering, Scrum focuses primarily on the team and the prioritization of work. In practical application, I frequently see Scrum practices used to manage teams and workflow (and even organizational structure), and XP practices (like TDD, continuous builds,

continuous testing, and collective code ownership) used to improve the quality of the software itself.

2. XP manages the prioritization of features through constant communication with the "customer" (although the definition of *customer* is and must be loosely interpreted—imagine working on a popular software package that thousands of people buy when new releases are sent to the stores; who would your customer be under those conditions?). Scrum assigns *total* responsibility for representing the customer, the market, and the business to a single role: the Product Owner. This makes the Product Owner solely responsible for the profitability of the product and streamlines the decision-making process with regard to content, value, and feature prioritization.

HOW DO YOU HANDLE MULTIPLE-TEAM COORDINATION IN SCRUM?

The Scrum framework puts a high priority on self-managing and self-organizing teams. As a result, it can be easy to forget to ensure that teams keep talking and that self-organization across teams is just as effective as self-organization within teams. Built into Scrum, but frequently misunderstood, is the concept of the Scrum of Scrums (SoS), a mechanism that provides for multiteam coordination and alignment. In most literature, including the material that "officially" (for lack of a better term) describes Scrum, the utility of the SoS is poorly explored.

For the purposes of this book, I review the topic in sufficient detail to fully answer the question that heads this section. Let us look at the SoS concept, what it is, how it works, and the various modes in which it can be used to support multiple-team coordination.

Scrum of Scrums

The fundamental concept behind the SoS is that two or more Scrum teams, at a frequency of once a week to once a day, gather their technical leads together to discuss the activities of their respective teams and to determine what, if any, changes in planning are necessary. Generally, the scope of what is discussed in an SoS is limited to related Product

Backlog items that are being built simultaneously by multiple Scrum teams.

SoS teams are formed by Scrum teams that have committed to completing Product Backlog items that are closely related to other Product Backlog items that other Scrum teams are also committing to during the same Sprint. SoS teams are opportunistic in nature, existing only when needed and dissolving when the need has passed.

If necessary, multiple SoS teams can exist simultaneously, consisting of representatives of different Scrum teams and focusing on different Product Backlog items.

Essentially, the SoS is a reflection of the self-organizing characteristics of the Scrum team taken "up" one level hierarchically. The SoS makes decisions within the scope of their purview, and the individual Scrum teams respond accordingly.

At these meetings, issues are discussed; decisions are made regarding how each team will proceed. The breadth and depth of the discussion are not bounded; therefore, a significant amount of cross-team coordination can take place during the SoS. Following the meeting, each team's representative communicates back to their team all pertinent information.

The standard SoS, then, is ideal for managing technical and procedural coordination related to specific Product Backlog items between multiple Scrum teams. But the SoS can also be used on a more practical level. This version of the SoS is called the coordinating Scrum of Scrums (CSoS) and is discussed next.

Coordinating Scrum-of-Scrums (CSoS)

The CSoS is similar to the "standard" SoS in form, but the purpose is a little different. In the standard SoS, teams get together to coordinate on one or two closely related backlog items. In the CSoS, multiple teams that find themselves frequently working on related software hold the CSoS as a standing meeting, usually right after the teams' Daily Scrum meetings.

In this arrangement, the CSoS acts as a coordination point for the teams. The team members who attend the CSoS then review what each team is doing and, based on how the teams have to work together, make decisions that they then take back to their teams to execute.

HOW DOES A SCRUM TEAM SELF-ORGANIZE WITH REGARD TO ASSIGNING TASKS?

While there are no specific rules in Scrum regarding the assignment of tasks to individuals, there are definitely many different views on the topic. Some teams believe that every task should be assigned to a specific team member from the point that the task is created during Sprint Planning. These teams say that they cannot estimate the size of a task unless they know who is going to actually do it. In addition, they say that, since everyone on the team has a specific skill set and expertise, it is pretty obvious who is going to work on which task anyway. I would like to suggest that this school of thought, outside the simplest Scrum team and the most basic product, actually demonstrates a real lack of understanding of Scrum and agile development and how they work.

In my opinion, tasks need not be assigned to anyone on the team until such time as a team member begins working on the task. But first, let us go back to why I believe the previously stated approach demonstrates a lack of understanding of Scrum and agile. First, let us address the belief that a task cannot be estimated unless you know who is going to work on it.

When a Scrum team creates the Sprint Backlog, the tasks on the backlog are created so that the team has a record of the things that they have to do to satisfy the commitment they make with the Product Owner during Sprint Planning. Further, the tasks are given estimates of completion in terms of hours so that the team, in modifying those hours each day, can generate a Sprint Burndown chart and thus track their progress during the Sprint. This means that the tasks, not the estimates, are used to identify the extent of the commitment to the Product Owner. Last, the estimate of any task is adjusted each day that the task is in progress to reflect the number of remaining hours of work according to the person or persons working on the task. So, not only does the task estimate play almost no role in determining the Sprint Goals, the estimate is changed to reflect actual remaining hours based on whomever is doing it—an inaccurate estimate based on the expectation that someone else will work on the task until corrected within the first 24 hours of the task being in progress.

As for the thought that task assignment is fairly predetermined because of skill set, I would counter that this argument does not reflect the possibilities for pairing with another developer to share or learn more information or reflect an understanding of highly collaborative teams where *who* works on a task is not nearly as important as working together to complete the backlog item.

Self-organization is a term we use to describe one of the defining principles of a Scrum team. It means that a team will decide how they want to solve a specific problem and will determine among themselves how they will create the solution. It is during the building of the solution that tasks are assigned to one or more team members. However, it is not considered best practice to attempt to "solve" all of the problems in the Sprint at the same time. Good development practices suggest that it is actually best only to work on one or two of the team's backlog items at any one time, completing one before starting another. This being true, it would follow that tasks are not assigned until the team decides to begin work on the backlog items.

To answer the question that began this section of the guide, I believe that the best way to handle task assignment is to do it right before you begin working on a backlog item. Therefore, tasks are not preassigned but rather assigned at the time the backlog items are begun.

DOES SWARMING ON SMALL STORIES INCREASE OR DECREASE PRODUCTIVITY?

There is absolutely no doubt in my mind that swarming on proper-size stories (that is, a well-understood story that should take two or three team members less than a week to build) will increase productivity. While I have no formal studies to prove this, I have personally watched the velocity of Scrum teams double and even triple as a result of proper-size stories and effective swarming. Now, having said that, let us talk about swarming. Then we will talk about why it works.

Science has, for years, highlighted the power of teamwork as a method for getting a lot of work accomplished in incredibly short periods of time. They use the examples of bees, ants, and birds. The bees, while having a few prescribed roles, work without supervision in a way that seems like every bee knows what to do without being told. Likewise with ants, who work together constantly in what seems like a chaotic mess, while clearly accomplishing goals that benefit the entire colony. Migratory birds, as well, can be seen flying in the well-known "V" formation, always knowing where they are going, always knowing when to take breaks, and constantly shifting which bird is flying in the point position to avoid getting too tired. These creatures do not make detailed plans regarding their itinerary or their goals; they do it because that is what they do.

Humans exhibit somewhat similar behavior in wartime maneuvers when they organize themselves into small groups, each group with a specific goal and a plan (and the understanding that most plans undergo constant change and reevaluation of the window once the battle is joined). These small groups, acting fairly autonomously to achieve their shared goals, can accomplish incredible feats against all odds.

All of these—bees, ants, birds, soldiers—exhibit characteristics of what is known as a *complex adaptive system*. A complex adaptive system, defined briefly, is one in which common goals are shared, but the process by which the goal is achieved is empirical. In other words, a complex adaptive system works by taking an action, examining the resulting environment, deciding what to do next, and then taking the next step. In addition, the goal frequently has a time component to it: The bees, ants, and birds need to achieve their goal before winter weather sets in; soldiers need to achieve their objective within a given timeframe, or the enemy might resupply or reposition, making hard-fought gains useless. This continuous process of action and feedback results in the appearance of chaotic behavior that is continuously aimed and re-aimed at accomplishing the team's goal. Bees continually adjust their pollen-gathering activities based on weather, safety, and quantity of available flowers. Ants modify their behavior based on weather, safety, and available food sources. Birds are also affected by weather, safety, and food. Soldiers, having much more complex goals (which, to add to the complexity, can change during the battle), modify their behavior based on weather, safety, supplies, enemy position and strength, time of day, and much more.

Scrum teams are examples of complex adaptive systems. They have a predetermined goal (the Sprint Goal), they have a predetermined timeframe (the Sprint), and they are continuously checking their current situation and adapting their activities appropriately. However, Scrum teams do not embrace complex adaptive system behavior on their own. Inappropriate behavior, such as the team not working as a team but rather as a group of individuals, will cause their behavior to be less reactive to empirical considerations and, on average, perform more poorly than a team that leverages empiricism. When the team does, in fact, collaborate continuously, embracing empiricism, they are said to be "swarming."

When a Scrum team swarms, its behavior changes radically. While you may, at times, see team members working independently, you will more often than not see team members working in small groups of three or four. While one team member might be writing code, the one sitting next to him or her is writing the tests that validate the code, and the one sitting next to them is updating the functional specifications to keep up with the changes that all three team members agreed to only an hour before. Later that day, after the specification changes are done and reviewed with the other two team members, the team member who updated the specifications will be joining another group of team members on the other side of the team room to help them. This seemingly unplanned "chaos" (defined as such because, while pursuing a specific goal, the patterns exhibited are, for the most part, unpredictable) actually works to bring the right people (and the right minds) to the right problem at the right time. The focus and innovative responses created by working in this manner tend to spawn the high performance that we all have been looking for in our teams for many years.

So, why does swarming work? Well, again, I am not aware of any formal studies done in this area, but the characteristics of a swarm that make it so effective in nature also appear in a Scrum team that employs swarming. The characteristics of a swarm and how it may be observed in a Scrum team are as follows:

- Scalability: A swarming team can scale easily, without changing how it works. We see this in a limited way in Scrum teams because teams themselves are limited in their total size. Essentially, whether I have five people on my team forming two small swarms or the maximum of nine people on my team forming two or three swarms, how they work does not change. Each person in the swarm works together, usually side by side, to get the work done.
- Parallel activity: In a swarming team, individuals can move from swarm to swarm as needed to maximize their utilization and to put the right skills in the right place. There is no specific plan for this; it simply happens when the swarms realize (through discussion, often identified during the Daily Scrum) that they need different skills in different places. Since all of the swarms belong to one team and the entire team shares the same goals, the prioritization of the goals helps to drive the skills-sharing decision process.

- Fault tolerance: In a swarming team, no one person can cause a failure across the team. Individuals not succeeding in one swarm can be moved to another swarm and their skills applied in a different manner. Likewise, no single individual can threaten the failure of a backlog item because the team can respond to a perceived potential failure much faster than if the work were being done by individuals, who may hide their failures behind weekly status reports until it is too late to recover.

When swarming, the team often divides into two swarms, each swarm focused on a different backlog item. Team members move freely, back and forth between the swarms as needed to get the work done. In addition, Scrum teams that swarm tend to only have two backlog items in progress at the same time, preferring to finish a backlog item completely before moving to start another. While this is not technically an aspect of swarming, keeping the team's work in progress to a minimum does help the team improve their focus while lessening both cost and risk during the Sprint.

If you want to get swarming working on your Scrum teams but you are not quite sure how to make it happen, start with these two simple rules:

- No one on the team works by themselves, and
- The team should not have more than two backlog items in progress at the same time.

These two rules will get your team started. The team will still need some coaching; if you really want swarming to work, you need a team that is both collaborative (they *want* to work together) and motivated (they *want* to build what they are building). Much of this will also come with time and experience.

SCRUMMASTERS: TECHNICAL BACKGROUND OR PROJECT MANAGEMENT BACKGROUND?

The answer to the question of whether ScrumMasters need a technical background or a project management background is going to be one of those thoroughly disappointing answers. Ready? Here it comes: It depends. Now, having provided the ultimate nonanswer as an answer, let me explain why.

A good ScrumMaster has (in part) the ability to keep the team focused, to make sure everybody is getting done what they said they needed to do, to clear obstacles that are keeping people from getting stuff done, and to make sure that the Scrum framework is properly supported and practiced. Nowhere in the definition of the ScrumMaster does it say that he or she has a technical understanding of the material being built. I acted as a ScrumMaster for a team for which I was familiar with the product but had no idea how it was built. Could I have been better with a technical background? Yes. In fact, this was why I learned about Java coding—I got tired of asking my team what they were talking about. It also, sometimes, made it easier for me to relate to others when I needed to take care of obstacles that were of a technical nature. I could have pulled it off without the technical knowledge, but it was better with it.

Nowhere in the definition of a ScrumMaster does it say that he or she should have a project management background. But, the background I already possessed helped me understand how to communicate my Scrum team's status to others and how to communicate with other project managers who were not working with Scrum teams.

What a good ScrumMaster really needs to be able to do has nothing to do with technical knowledge or project management knowledge. Both are useful, but both can be learned while one is already a ScrumMaster. The key skills for a ScrumMaster do not come from a particular area or department in your organization. You might find better ScrumMasters in your project management organization (PMO) than in your development ranks; then again, you might not. What makes a good ScrumMaster can be found in all sorts of people. To boil it all down, when you are looking for a good ScrumMaster, you are looking for someone who

- **Cares** about the organization, about the product, and mostly about the people
- **Communicates** effectively to all sorts of people and teams
- **Coordinates** well across multiple groups and multiple concerns
- **Cooperates** well with other people, subordinating his or her own goals for those of the team

Having technical knowledge or project management knowledge can help—but only in addition to these traits, not as a replacement for them.

SCRUM MEANS LESS DOCUMENTATION—WHAT SHOULD I DO WITH EXISTING DOCUMENTATION?

Actually, Scrum does not say a single word about documentation in the entire method. To decide what to do about documentation, we have to go back to the agile principles to make a decision, and even that is only partial.

From an agile development perspective, the manifesto is the *only* item that actually even references documentation. Even then, the reference is indirect. The agile manifesto says, roughly, that "we value working software over comprehensive documentation." From this, we can assume that, while there is value in documentation, there is more value in working software. We can use this as our first clue with regard to documentation.

One of the agile principles says, "Simplicity—the art of maximizing the amount of work not done—is essential." This is a slightly backward way of suggesting that simplicity is highly desired in agile development. The focus on simplicity is reinforced by the TDD practice of XP, in which refactoring of the code, a step aimed at simplifying the code, is a required part of the overall practice. In addition, we can look at the practices of backlog prioritization and user story slicing—which together reduce the functional size of stories and prioritize the more valuable ones higher—as evidence of the focus of agile development on value. If agile development places importance on simple, value-driven software, and software is more highly valued than documentation, it is not a difficult leap to suggest that documentation in an agile development environment would also be driven by simplicity and value.

While there is not much guidance in agile development with regard to documentation, the idea that documentation should be driven by simplicity and value makes a lot of sense. To that end, there are some practices that I routinely advise my customers to use with regard to their documentation. These practices, when followed, tend to reduce the amount of time that a team spends writing documentation, which of course should give them more time for writing new software. The practices are as follows:

1. **Write only documentation that you know you need.** I have run across many instances of documentation plans and documentation templates that follow one simple rule: the more, the better. Unfortunately, while this may be true in payroll checks and sunny days, it is the absolute opposite of reality in software development.

I cannot count the number of times I have walked past shelves of "write once, read never" documentation. You can identify it easily enough; it is never removed from its wrappings, and if it is, it is never read. When planning and writing documentation, focus on the documentation that actually has an audience—someone who will actually need or want to read it. I do not just mean finding an audience manual by manual and specification by specification; I also suggest looking at the sections within the documents and specifications. If you cannot figure out a reasonable scenario in which someone might use the specification or portion thereof, do not write it. Last, there may become an instance when you cannot figure out if someone might need the documentation. In this instance, my recommendation would be that you do a little more digging; ask around in various departments that use or somehow provide services around your product; ask quality management if you have one; ask a few auditors if you work in a regulated environment. In the end, if someone does not say, "Yes, definitely I need it," *do not write it.* (I know that sounds drastic, but you will save a lot of valuable time not writing things you do not need, and the odds are probably in your favor. In the off chance that you do, in fact, need the missing documentation, you can probably write it after the fact at little additional cost. But, going with the odds here could save you hours or even hundreds of hours.)

2. **Write specifications based on the product, not the project.** When writing specifications, many organizations take the shortcut and simply write new functional and detailed specifications for each new feature that is developed (I am guilty of this myself). In the end, however, you wind up with an extensive library of disjointed specifications, none of which truly give you a clear understanding of your product code because it is all jumbled from one specification to the next. I call this "the specification jungle" (Figure 12.1).

My recommendation for internal specifications (functional specification, detailed design specifications, database schema specifications) is to make them more comprehensive and then use version control to keep track of the changes that are introduced on a project-by-project basis or even a Sprint-by-Sprint basis. For example, assume we are building a student registration system for a large university. The registration system is grouped around seven major functional areas and, for each area, there is a set of functional and design specifications.[1] The areas are

FIGURE 12.1
A "specification jungle" that makes impossible a comprehensive picture of the actual state of a product.

- Student management
- Class management
- Faculty management
- Scholarship management
- Architecture
- Client services—common services for displaying information
- Security—authentication, authorization, auditing

Now, before the first Sprint started, we worked on an architecture definition document. So, that and the Product Backlog were what we took into the first Sprint.

During the very first Sprint of the very first version of the product, the Scrum teams worked primarily on architecture and the beginnings of the client services and security. This would allow us to provide the beginnings of a log-in screen (which was important since we always want to have customer-facing functionality coming out of every Sprint). So, by the time the Sprint ended, the teams finished versions of the following:

- Security Functional Specification v1.0.1
- Security Detailed Design Specification v1.0.1
- Client Services Functional Specification v1.0.1

- Client Service Detailed Design Specification v1.0.1
- Architecture Design Specification v1.0.1

In each specification, the "v1.0" references both the version and release of the software. The final ".1" references the number of the Sprint in the version/release. Moving forward into the next Sprint, the teams complete more of the architecture, client services, and security systems and begin working on the faculty management pieces of the product. As you might expect, the following specifications were either created or updated during the second Sprint:

- Security Functional Specification v1.0.2
- Security Detailed Design Specification v1.0.2
- Client Services Functional Specification v1.0.2
- Client Services Detailed Design Specification v1.0.2
- Architecture Design Specification v1.0.2
- Faculty Management Functional Specification v1.0.2
- Faculty Management Detailed Design Specification v1.0.2

In these specifications, the final ".2" refers, again, to the Sprint number. Note that the faculty management specifications, created for the first time in this Sprint, do not start at "v1.0.1". Their release identifier is based on the Sprint in which the specification is created or modified.

As development continues forward, the specifications are given a new version designation every time a new version of the specification is created or modified. By the time the project is finished, after nine Sprints, each specification has a version designation that is somewhere between v1.0.1 and v1.0.9. When the next project begins, the version designations begin at v1.1.1 (version 1, release 1, sprint 1) and increase from there.

As a result of this approach, we get three distinct advantages. First, we have a state of the product as it exists at the end of each Sprint and at the end of each project. Second, we have specifications that always represent a comprehensive description of each piece of the product. Third, it is both easier to write and easier to learn from specifications written in this manner.

Finally, as far as existing documentation or specifications you might already have, in my experience you have three options: (a) leave the documents as is and start building new specifications with your next project,

(b) run a short project to combine all of the existing specifications into a library as discussed, or (c) do both, starting with a whole new set of specifications, but retrofitting the old specifications into the new ones a little at a time.

REFERENCE

Schiel, James A. 2010. *Enterprise-Scale Agile Software Development*. Boca Raton, FL: CRC Press.

ENDNOTE

1. Yes, there might be more, but I want to keep the example as simple as possible.

13

Using Scrum

INTRODUCTION

Scrum is an agile development framework focusing on collaborative teams of developers who build software in close contact with someone who knows exactly what the software feature needs to be able to do. Using empirical process control, Scrum teams set short-term goals and then modify their approach day after day until they attain the best results that they are able during the iteration time box.

This chapter looks at some of the common questions about Scrum and how it works. As there seem to be many different interpretations of what is and is not Scrum,[1] you may encounter some differences in thought or approach. Do not let that bother you. Read what you find here with an open mind and use what you can to improve things in the real world.

HOW MANY SCRUM TEAMS CAN A PRODUCT OWNER HAVE?

The Scrum method does not specify a limit for the number of teams that a Product Owner can have. Given that a Product Owner is responsible for a product, it is clearly conceivable that it may require more than one team to create what the Product Owner desires. That said, I have rarely seen a Product Owner be able to work with more than three Scrum teams without significant difficulty maintaining. Prioritizing a backlog is difficult enough; doing so while attending Sprint Planning meetings, Sprint Review meetings, Sprint Retrospective meetings, and backlog grooming workshops for more than three teams is simply too much. It can be done, but it is not easy.

When dealing with multiple Scrum teams, the problems the Product Owner faces fall into three categories:

- Scheduling
- Backlog management
- Team interaction

We look at all three problems and some of the possible solutions in the paragraphs that follow.

Scheduling

Scheduling is probably the most obvious and the easiest to explain. Every Scrum team performs a Sprint Planning meeting, a Sprint Review meeting, Daily Scrum meetings, and several grooming and design meetings during every Sprint. This means that, at a minimum, a Product Owner can spend up to 35 hours per 4-week Sprint with just a single team (and even that is too little time for a team). Add a second, third, or even fourth team, and there is extremely little time left for the Product Owner to manage the backlog, talk with stakeholders, and talk with customers.

One potential solution to the scheduling problem is to stagger or "shift" (Schiel 2010, 223) the Sprints across the teams that work with the same Product Owner. In this practice, one or two of the teams start their Sprints on Thursdays, while a third team starts their Sprint on Wednesdays (the Sprints, of course, end on different days of the week as well). This tends to spread out the Sprint Planning and Sprint Review meetings, giving the Product Owner more opportunities to attend these critical meetings.

Backlog Management

To work with a Scrum team, the Product Owner must keep the backlog prioritized and ready in advance of the Scrum team's grooming efforts. This takes a considerable amount of effort on the part of the Product Owner. Some of the effort can be alleviated by pairing one or more analysts with the Product Owner to communicate the Product Owner's wishes to the Scrum teams. However, this merely replaces the effort of working with the Scrum teams with the effort of working with the analysts; for this to work effectively, the analysts must already have a good understanding of the product in question as well as the Product Owner's vision for the product.

Team Interactions

In many instances when the Product Owner works with multiple teams, it is because those teams are working on a related portion of the product or on related functionality. This means that the Product Owner will likely have to deal with issues of functional or technical interaction across and between his or her teams. This makes the work the teams are doing a little harder as they will often have to plan larger solutions together to execute the smaller solutions based on backlog item by backlog item.

Imagine, for example, three teams working together on a student registration system for a large university. As those teams work on how to register students within a particular school in the university, how to move students between schools, and how to resolve duplicate students in multiple schools, they must work together to ensure that a larger solution guides all of the smaller solutions. The easiest way to solve these issues is to do something that is part of Scrum and to add some pieces that are not. First, the Product Owner needs to encourage Scrums of Scrums during all Sprints. This will keep the teams coordinating and collaborating as they work on similar or connected stories. Here are some more ideas:

1. Encourage movement of team members between the teams as needed. Let the teams decide how to do it. The more the teams act together as a sort of megateam, the more the movement of personnel between the teams will keep any loss of productivity from the changing of members to a minimum. From a broader perspective, the more you allow the teams to self-coordinate, the more they will be able to do.

2. Hold joint Sprint Reviews. Bring all of the teams together during the Sprint Review and have each team review what they finished during the Sprint. You hold the review pretty much as normal, but those in each team act as stakeholders for the work of the others.

3. Hold joint backlog grooming workshops with a limited number of people from each team. These sessions would not replace the team grooming sessions but rather would give each team a forum to work together, slice the backlog items across team responsibilities or boundaries (if they exist), and learn about the backlog items from the Product Owner in advance of the team-specific meetings.

WHAT DO YOU DO WHEN THE PRODUCT OWNER WILL NOT ENGAGE?

It is, unfortunately, all too common for Scrum teams to have Product Owners who refuse to actually spend time with the Scrum team for any of a number of reasons, including

- "I don't have time."
- "I wrote down what I wanted; just do it."
- "You should already know what I want."

The variations on these excuses are endless, but they usually boil down to one of them. Unfortunately, whatever the reason, the disengaged Product Owner is essentially robbing the team of direction in terms of functionality and priority. So, the team does not know what to build— anything they do could be a waste of time. In reality, how the situation is handled depends on the team's ability to work without a Product Owner as well as the desire of the organization to do Scrum properly, or just say they are doing it. As far as Scrum is concerned, you really only have one option:

- **Get another Product Owner.** Someone who cannot or will not fulfill the Product Owner responsibilities must be replaced as quickly as possible. In fact, I have worked with organizations where managers stepped in to play the Product Owner role and then did not engage with the teams because they were too busy being both a Product Owner and a manager. This is exactly the time when you want to suggest that the person who is currently the Product Owner should *not* be the Product Owner. They could be a stakeholder instead, providing valuable input to the Product Owner.

If you are willing to look beyond Scrum, you might also try the following (although I guarantee that nothing will be as effective as replacing the current Product Owner with someone who will do the job properly):

- **Create a Product Owner on the team.** If your team has someone who is experienced with the product, you might be able to identify someone on the team who can prioritize the work and explain it well enough that the team can build it. This person would also have the unlucky responsibility of working with the former "Product Owner" (if possible) to continue to align on priority and functional description.

- **Work closely with the end users.** If your Product Owner cannot or will not give you the functional details you need, find one or more end users you can work with who can and will. You can get these users involved in backlog grooming, Sprint Planning, and the Sprint in much the same way you would involve a Product Owner.

In the end, all of the available options are about replacing the reluctant Product Owner with one who might be able to do the job satisfactorily (with another team member or with end users).

WHAT TOOLS ASSIST IN A SCRUM PROJECT?

The question of proper tooling is one that comes up repeatedly. Since the earliest days of the popular use of Scrum, as choices grew from one or two tools to literally hundreds with differing purposes, the question has simply become increasingly confusing. The best answer I can provide on this particular topic comes in two pieces: First, I share some honest experience I have had with various tools; second, I provide some serious advice you should consider before doing anything else with a tool.

Tooling and Tools

I am not going to attempt to provide detailed accounts of the tool vendors, their history, and their strategies. In this section, I simply want to provide my impression of the tools. I should also note that my examination of the tools here is neither exhaustive nor extensive.

Backlog Management—Tools can help you keep track of your backlog, your Sprints, and your progress. These tools generally support backlog prioritization, some form of story slicing, building and tracking of Sprint backlogs, and charting for Sprint and release progress. Some tools provide some fundamental Sprint management support (planning a Sprint, reviewing/closing a Sprint), some security to keep the wrong people from accessing the wrong data, and some fundamental retrospective support.

- **VersionOne**—A good, powerful tool for the large-scale (10 or more teams) environment. Most of the functions are reasonably easy to use and easy to understand, but it is a little overpowered for the small environment. The tool does a good job at helping the Scrum team manage the Sprint by providing good planning and review functions. It also provides something that has become the expected, ubiquitous capability: the online task board.

- **Rally**—Like VersionOne, a market leader in this particular market niche. Rally has a powerful tool, good for both the large and small environment. It can also be complicated to use, and it takes some getting used to. The tool provides good planning and review functions as well as, yes, the online task board.

- **ScrumWorks**—Unlike Rally and VersionOne, this tool is not trying to be an agile development tool; it is trying to be a Scrum development tool. ScrumWorks has strong planning, review, and task board capabilities as well as a simple-to-use user UI paradigm. The biggest challenge of ScrumWorks is the fact that it is struggling to keep up in the marketplace. Where Rally and VersionOne took advantage of deeper pocketbooks, ScrumWorks' original parent company, Danube Technologies, kept itself "in the family" and had to make do with what they had. Still, the tool is affordable and worth using.[2]

- **Microsoft Team Foundation Server (TFS)**—At its root, TFS provides back-end services accessible via exposed Web services that can be used to build front-end applications. As a result, most organizations cannot truly make use of TFS as a backlog management tool without installing one or more plug-ins that provide the "Scrum" front-end appearance. So, how good the tool is (as well as how long it takes to make it usable and how much it costs) depends on the plug-ins that are available when you decide to install and use TFS. My experience with this tool so far is that it scales well and performs well, regardless of the plug-ins, but that none of the plug-ins is really as good as what VersionOne, Rally, and ScrumWorks provide.

- **GreenHopper**—Just as TFS uses plug-ins to provide Scrum-like functionality, GreenHopper is a front end or plug-in to the JIRA product. Both GreenHopper and JIRA are provided by Atlassian.

GreenHopper provides good backlog management functionality and good reporting. Unfortunately, it is weak in terms of story slicing (it does not actually seem to support it); it also does not support Sprint Planning or Sprint Review very well. However, it does support the online task board, if properly configured.

Source Code Control—Tools that help you manage versions of software are extremely important for an agile development team. The necessity to be able to modify code, test it, add it to the rest of the tested product, and then rapidly and efficiently test it with the entire product is an absolute requirement. Luckily, the number of useful tools here provide a much shorter list.

- **Clearcase**—A strong, solid, full-functioned tool with considerable support and the ability to scale. It can be a little difficult to set up but is well worth it once it is properly configured. It is solid, strong, and flexible. However, I believe that Microsoft may be putting increased focus on TFS for source code control, so Clearcase could be seeing the end of the road in the not-too-distant future.

- **Subversion**—This is a good tool with considerable community support and more than enough functionality for the small- to medium-size development shop. It is also nicely integrated into the Eclipse and Netbeans development environments. Subversion also seems to enjoy ongoing development activities (unlike CVS) and has found a partner in Apache.

- **Concurrent Versions System (CVS)**—This is another good tool with considerable community support and enough functionality for the small-to-medium development shop. Like Subversion, CVS is nicely integrated into Netbeans, although not so well into Eclipse. On the downside, however, there does not seem to be a lot of new development going on with CVS (as of the writing of this book, the most recent stable version of CVS was 1.11.23, released on May 8, 2008).

Continuous Build and Testing Tools—A mainstay of agile development, continuous integration is key to ensuring that software quality is maintained during the development process. Once again, there are a few tools that seem to have bubbled to the top and are in consistent use by agile development organizations. All of these tools are highly configurable, have strong support for build and test operations, have easy-to-understand UIs, and provide support for e-mailing on predetermined conditions.

- **CruiseControl**—An open-source project with lots of plug-ins make this tool very extensible, but if you have a problem, getting help in the form of documentation or program support could be an issue.
- **Hudson**—Also an open-source project with lots of plug-ins, it is a little easier to find help when you need it, however. The Hudson online materials seem to be better maintained.
- **Bamboo**—You have to pay for this one, but as with most of the Atlassian software, this product is fairly well maintained and up to date.
- **Microsoft TFS**—If you are a Microsoft shop, this is probably the tool you will want to go with. It is well integrated with Visual Studio and comes with abundant documentation and support.

Automated Unit Testing—As with continuous builds, automated testing is an absolute requirement. While there are a number of different tools that suit this need, the n-unit (c-unit, j-unit, py-unit, phpunit, etc.) family seems to provide the right mix of versatility and simplicity. Most integrated development environments (IDEs), like Eclipse, Visual Studio, and Netbeans, support n-unit testing easily.

Automated Acceptance and Integration Testing—Building on our unit tests are acceptance (functional) tests that go a step beyond unit tests in ensuring that each function that we build works properly. Integration tests go a step beyond to ensure that the new functionality "plays nicely" with the rest of the product. The tools that I have found work the best in this environment are as follows:

- **Fitnesse**—I absolutely love this tool for its simplicity. This is a wiki-like tool that allows you to document your software, write your tests, and run them all from the same location. Tests are created on each Fitnesse page in terms of tables that can both submit data to the application and analyze the response to that data. Pages can be hierarchically ordered to allow for packaging of tests. Packages can be brought together with other pages just by referencing the pages with the desired tests. The only downside to this tool (and I am not really sure it is a downside) is that your developers will have to write simple "fixtures" that interface between the Fitnesse page and the application under test; however, the fixtures are easy to write and can be quite flexible.

- **Selenium**—Another of my favorite tools, Selenium allows browser-based UI testing. What makes it even better, in my opinion, is that it effectively integrates with Fitnesse, allowing you to control most of the automated testing from one location, Fitnesse, even when the tests are being executed by two tools, Fitnesse and Selenium. In addition, both Selenium and Fitnesse can be run from CruiseControl and Hudson (in all likelihood, Bamboo can run it as well).

A Cautionary Word about Backlog Management Tools

The thing with backlog management tools is that, while they do a good job of helping us get things done, they are often implemented before the organization, and especially the teams, have a clear understanding of what value they bring and how they can be leveraged to help the organization. Even when a salesperson provides an excellent statement of value and multiple case studies to back up statements, being convinced that a tool can provide value is very different from knowing how to realize that value through the use of the tool.

As an example, I have seen many Scrum teams be given a backlog management tool like VersionOne, Rally, or ScrumWorks (it is not about the tool). We teach them how to use the tool and show them how the task board works. Then, we spend the next 6 months reminding them to use the board, reminding them to keep the board current, reminding them how to use the task board from day to day. When I compare this to teams that work with a physical task board and without a backlog management tool for a few months, their attitude when they get an online version of the tool is much different—they use the tool more effectively (although many teams actually see the tool as a hindrance at this point, rather than an improvement). What I have learned is this: While tools make things simpler, they do not teach values or principles.

Agile development is about "individuals and interactions." You cannot teach the disciplines, attitudes, and values of agile development through tools. Your best bet when teaching a new team is to teach them without tools first. Let them build and maintain their backlog on index cards; let them build and maintain their task board. This is how they learn concepts and principles. This is how they learn *why* things work and how to use them. This is how they learn how to leverage Scrum and agile development. Once they have integrated these concepts into their daily practices, feel free to implement tools that help the teams do things faster or more efficiently.

DOES SCRUM WORK BY ITSELF?

Scrum has no prerequisites—except people. Scrum can be used without any other changes to engineering practices or engineering infrastructure, but you should expect your success with agile development to be limited if the only thing you are doing is Scrum. While Scrum will help by prioritizing the work to be done and will help the team to organize itself to get the work done, there are many *very* important things that Scrum does not do. For example, Scrum can help your team to work on the most valuable stuff first, but it cannot help you improve your product quality if your development standards are poor or if you have no automated tests to verify the quality of your code. Scrum does an excellent job of helping to clarify acceptance criteria, but it will not help you if your team does not have the skills they need to get the job done or if your Product Owners do not truly understand the customers or the market.

If you do not have a good, solid engineering infrastructure and good engineering practices in place, the ability of Scrum to help you build a valuable, high-quality product is limited at best.

On the other hand, if you happen to be using Scrum to plan your group's annual banquet or in a human resources department to keep your group communicating and focused on the highest priorities of your department, Scrum may be just what you need to create an effective, high-performance team.

WHAT IS SPRINT ZERO, AND HOW DO I USE IT?

"Sprint Zero" (discussed also in Chapter 3, "Release Planning and 'Iteration Zero'") is a commonly used device in Scrum-based projects. Occurring as the first Sprint in the project, Sprint Zero denotes a period of time during which the following activities usually take place:

- The product backlog is readied. This also involves an initial selection of the scope of the product backlog that is anticipated to be done for the current project (frequently called the "release backlog").
- Resources are identified for Scrum teams. This step often waits until after the scope is selected in the previous step. This makes it easier to determine which skills are needed and in what supply. During this

step, new Scrum teams might be created, old teams might be dissolved, or the teams might be left exactly as they were before.

- The development infrastructure is established. This may consist of product staging environments (development, test, integration, and production), source code control environments, and database environments, among many other possibilities.

- Some high-level evaluation of the backlog items identified for the release might be performed. This does not happen all the time, however. This step is usually reserved for projects for which there might be a need to upgrade hardware or software used by development or advanced notice of certain requirements is critical. This is typical in environments in which an agile project needs a deliverable from a group, department, or company still doing waterfall development and requires considerable up-front otiose in order to commit.

- A detailed grooming of the "top" of the backlog is performed to ready the backlog items for the first development Sprint. This step is done when the project team feels that the items on the backlog require some initial discussion by the Scrum teams for the teams to plan their first Sprint effectively. It is also acceptable, if the team is capable, to discuss, groom, and plan simultaneously during Sprint Planning, alleviating the need for additional grooming.

- The architecture definition is written or revised (depending on the content of the release). This is a crucial step for *any* Scrum project in which a product is to be created or enhanced. Scrum teams need careful and consistent direction from their architects (or their architecture definition, or both) to build a product effectively. If there is confusion regarding what the architecture is supposed to do and how it is supposed to do it, the architecture definition should clear up the confusion.

- Project-wide training is performed for all teams and individuals who need it. This might involve training on how to be on a Scrum team, on the product to be built, or in the market for which the product is intended.

- The Sprint schedule is defined. For some organizations, this only involves setting the start date for the first Sprint and the desired date of completion so that the product can be shipped. In other organizations, we also have to determine the length of each Sprint and the length of the time in between Sprints.

All of these activities are crucial to starting a Scrum project. In some projects, they take place in a Sprint Zero, and in others, they are done either in a period of time prior to the beginning of the project or during the first Sprint of the project.

Personally, my own objection to the Sprint Zero label is that the period of time called Sprint Zero is not a Sprint at all. There is often no Product Backlog, no Sprint Backlog, no ScrumMaster, no Sprint Planning meeting, no Daily Scrums—in short, there is nothing about Sprint Zero that is actually a Sprint. In my mind, if it is not a Sprint, you should not call it a Sprint. You could, however, reasonably call this period of time a "Planning Iteration" or a "Preparatory Iteration" (although even calling the time period an "iteration" is pushing the limits of the definition of an iteration). To be fair, in some rare cases, I have heard of these preparatory Sprints actually being run as a Sprint (I have done so myself); in those cases, I have much less objection calling the Sprint a Sprint (whether it is zero, one, or "George"). As with many similar semantic arguments, call it whatever makes sense in your organization.

Whether you call it a Sprint, whether you manage it as a Sprint, the period of time just before a first development Sprint of a project, often called Sprint Zero, is a period of time when the content, schedule, architecture, staffing, and engineering infrastructure of the project are established.

WITHIN A PROJECT, CAN SPRINT LENGTHS BE DIFFERENT?

In general, changing Sprint lengths during a project is a bad idea. The reason for this is that much of the manner in which Scrum teams determine how much they can do during a Sprint is by comparison to previous Sprints. In other words, when a team successfully completes 15 story points in one Sprint and then proceeds to complete 17, 15, 14, and 16 story points during the next four Sprints, respectively (which gives them a velocity of 15 story points), they are fairly likely to complete something close to 15 story points in the next Sprint as well (yes, something could happen that causes the team to only get 11 story points instead, but the odds are against it).

This consistency in the amount of work that a team completes during a Sprint is, to a large degree, a factor of consistent Sprint length. As you might guess, a team that can get 15 story points of work done in one 2-week

Sprint will get more done in a 3-week Sprint, and even more done in a 4-week Sprint. So, if we keep using the same Sprint length, it is reasonably likely that the team will complete a similar amount of work each Sprint.

Teams do not reach a consistent velocity right away, though. During the first Sprint, not knowing how much work they can really do, a team is more likely to significantly overcommit or undercommit than to predict their velocity. During subsequent Sprints, the team will get increasingly better at predicting their velocity, assuming the Sprint length remains constant. If the Sprint length varies during a period, the team does not learn what their true velocity is. They end up guessing at the beginning of each Sprint without the benefit of past experience. In other words, if we go from 3-week Sprints at 15 story points to 2-week Sprints, should the team automatically assume 10 story points (two-thirds of 15)? They could do so, and load the Sprint accordingly, only to find that their actual velocity dropped to 8 story points.

The work that Scrum teams do does not fit evenly into each day of the Sprint. In other words, on day 3 of the Sprint, the team might get 75 hours of task work done. On the next day, that number might be 90; it might also easily be 35. Teams do not burn work down at a consistent rate during the Sprint. Some teams get faster during a Sprint, working their fastest near the end. Others work faster as the Sprint enters its second week and then begin to slow again during the last days of the Sprint. Indeed, some tasks may defy completion in a small number of days, particularly those tasks that rely on assistance or support from other project teams or other Scrum teams.

So, for a given team, 3 weeks might be a perfect time box for how the team works and the kind of work they do. Two weeks, however, may not give the team enough time to really hit their stride each Sprint.

Having said all that, there are two instances when varying the length of the Sprint can lead to better results (even if it does play havoc with the team's ability to commit to work during Sprint Planning). The first instance is when you have a new team and you are trying to figure out the more effective Sprint length for them to use. Then, you might want to start a team with a 4-week Sprint for a few Sprints, then adjust the length down to 3 weeks. Keep reducing the Sprint length down to either 2 or 1 weeks and then look at the average points per week at each Sprint length. The Sprint length that yields the greatest points per week might be the one you want to go with for this team. Keep in mind, of course, that two other possibilities are just as likely: (a) You should just let the team decide how long its Sprint should be, and (b) there may not be any choice to make if the organization has mandated a Sprint length to synchronize a number of Scrum teams.

The second instance when varying Sprint length can yield better results usually happens during a time in a large project when greater visibility of the condition of the product is desired. By shortening Sprints to 1 or 2 weeks and providing more opportunities to review the product, Product Owners and stakeholders get additional opportunities to see a working product and can prioritize the backlog based on the remaining time and the condition of the product (Are all of the tests passing? Is it performing properly?)

As an example, assume a 10-month project running on 4-week Sprints. During the last 2 months, however, the Sprints are shortened to 2 weeks. This gives the Product Owner and stakeholders an opportunity to see how the product is doing and make decisions based on the remaining work and the remaining time.

CAN I USE THE V MODEL IN MY SPRINTS?

Over the years, I have run into implementations of the V model of software development. This model is generally used in waterfall-type projects as it clearly delineates three separate but related phases in software development. The first phase is *project definition*, during which the operations, requirements, architecture, and detailed design are completed. The third phase is the phase for *project test and integration*, during which testing activities validate the pieces of the first phase. Between the two phases, the second phase is *implementation*, for which the V model contributes little (Figure 13.1).

Now, the ironic part of this particular story is that the V model talks about phases in a project, completely missing the fact that the relationships it is trying to draw between definition and testing are perfectly valid at the feature level. To put it in Scrum parlance, while I would never implement the V model on a Sprint (i.e., a week of analysis and definition, a week of design, a week of coding, and a week of testing), I can absolutely envision implementing the concepts discussed in the V model on every backlog item built by the Scrum team. Not that I would want Scrum teams to create tasks like "design this" or "test that," but the V model does give a good idea of what should happen to each

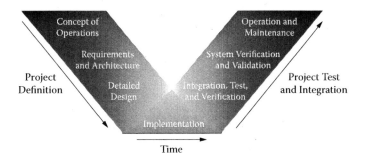

FIGURE 13.1

The V model of software development. The left, downward side describes analysis and design, which precede implementation. Implementation is at the bottom of the V. The right, upward side describes testing efforts, which follow implementation. Each item on the downward side corresponds to an item on the upward side. Specifically, requirements and architecture are the subjects of system verification and validation.

backlog item, from clarifying the requirements and architecture (during backlog grooming and Sprint Planning) to completing the design, implementation, integration testing, and system testing (during the Sprint). As well, it gives us a guide against which our teams should be creating test cases and writing tests. For example, the acceptance criteria on a backlog item should be paired with system and functional tests. The detailed design criteria should be paired with integration test cases.

So, while the V model is not truly useful in a Sprint, what it is trying to show us is useful and should be built into the development practices of every Scrum team that is writing software.

HOW DO YOU KEEP DAILY SCRUMS WORKING AFTER SEVERAL SPRINTS?

When holding Daily Scrum meetings, you may find that they lack "energy" after several Sprints. I have seen this happen, and if you are not careful, it could lead to the team getting less and less out of the meeting and putting more and more pressure on you, the ScrumMaster, to hold the meetings less frequently.

First, let us look at some of the symptoms of lackluster and functionally weak Daily Scrums.

1. They start late. People do not show up on time, so the meeting always starts late. When you ask why people are late, excuses range from getting stopped in the hallway to simply forgetting about the meeting.
2. They end in just a few minutes. You might think that a really fast Daily Scrum is a good thing, but the next time you are in one, at the end of the meeting consider what you learned about what the team was doing. Did you learn anything useful? Are you comfortable you know what everyone is up to? Are you comfortable that everyone on the team knows what everyone else is doing? Are the right issues being discussed by the team members who are affected by them? Think about it for a few minutes. Are you a little vague about all these issues?
3. Responses are brief, or you feel like you have to drag it out. People are not really interested in talking about what they are doing. In fact, you might even detect a lack of openness on the part of the team. They might be keeping information to themselves.
4. They degrade immediately into detailed technical discussions or arguments. People are not seeing the value in the Daily Scrum, so they have switched either to discussions that they see as more valuable (detailed technical discussions) or to discussions that allow them to blow off frustration since everyone is in the same place (arguments).

There are many different reasons why this might happen, and sometimes there are multiple reasons causing problems at the same time. You will have to examine each possibility, decide if it applies, and then decide what kind of solutions you want to try to see if it makes a difference. Here are some of the most likely causes:

1. **Lack of understanding:** The team does not understand the value and purpose in the Daily Scrum and does not see why they have to do it every day. To them, the Daily Scrum feels, at best, like overhead and, at worst, like micromanagement. Since they cannot see the value, they will push to discontinue the meeting and, failing that, to hold the meeting only a couple times a week.
   • **Solution:** Retrain—the team needs to understand that the fundamental underpinnings in Scrum are team self-organization and empirical process control. Self-organization requires that everyone on the team functions together to make decisions

that support achieving the Sprint goals. Empirical process control requires that the team be able to inspect the environment and adapt their planning on a daily basis. When requirements, priorities, the condition of the software product, and even the staffing of the team change, the team must be able to adapt to those changes quickly and efficiently. The Daily Scrum helps the team achieve the transparency necessary for inspection and adaptation to occur. When the nightly build fails, a critical team member is out sick, or a design decision ends up being the wrong decision, the team needs to be able to understand the changes in their environment rapidly and to respond to those changes quickly and effectively. Without the Daily Scrum, the team is partially blinded. Their effectiveness is reduced, and their ability to react quickly is hindered. When moving at the high velocity many Scrum teams achieve, partial blindness and slow reactions can lead to extremely poor results.

2. **Lack of collaboration:** The team does not get any value from the Daily Scrum because they are not working collaboratively. Typical complaints are that "the Daily Scrum is waste of time because what people are talking about has nothing to do with me." This is a sign of a serious problem. Scrum teams that just take backlog items off the Product Backlog and then work independently on the items are not Scrum teams. They are just groups of people. If you are looking to get benefit from the Scrum framework, you will not get much if your teams are working like this.

   • **Solution:** Your bigger problem here is not the Daily Scrum; it is how your team is working. For a team to truly be effective and achieve improved productivity, they need to start working together on backlog items. They need to collaborate. To achieve this, you will need to implement two changes to how you manage your Sprint.

   First, *no one is allowed to work on a backlog item alone.* This change ensures that the team starts working together, combining their talent, perspective, and intelligence for every problem. It works best when one individual on the team takes responsibility for a backlog item and then invites others to join him or her in getting it done. The spontaneously formed subteam then works together on the backlog item, working on the various tasks, deciding among themselves who should work on which task. The subteam usually works on the backlog item side by side, discussing and determining the solution as a team, and then writing test cases and code and updating specifications simultaneously. When required by the available skills, people on the Scrum can move between subteams (there are usually no more than two subteams in a proper size Scrum team). Even defects can support a multimember subteam; the subteam determines a solution and then writes code and tests and updates specifications at the same time.

Second, *no more than two backlog items may be in progress at the same time.* In other words, the third backlog item on the Sprint Backlog may not be started until one of the first two backlog items has been completely finished. This change accomplishes three goals: First, it ensures that no "undesirable" tasks are left until the end of the Sprint. Second, it moves the team's priority from getting tasks done to getting backlog items done. Third, it reduces the amount of work in progress, which in turn reduces risk and improves team focus and performance during the Sprint.

By implementing these changes, you will make it impossible for your team not to collaborate. The more they work together, the more the Daily Scrum will become an important part of their daily routine. Of course, if they refuse to try to work in this manner (and there will be all kinds of excuses, few of which will actually matter), you have a much bigger issue than the Daily Scrum. At this point, your question should be, "How do I get a group to be a Scrum team?"

3. **Feeling of being micromanaged:** Nothing kills the desire to be self-managing faster than the feeling that you are being watched and rated by management on a daily basis. I have seen far too many Daily Scrums with the ScrumMaster recording minutes on a laptop or a notepad. If you watch carefully, you will note in these situations that the conversation (defined by who is making eye contact with whom) is always between the team member and the ScrumMaster. You will also notice that, unless you happen to be a team member speaking at the time, no one else looks even remotely interested in what is being said. As a result, the Daily Scrum has actually morphed into a very inefficiently run status meeting, where everybody stays and waits their turn and leaves when the meeting is over.

- **Solution:** Stop treating the Daily Scrum meeting as if the conversation is between the ScrumMaster and the team member. It is not. The conversation should be between the team members. Stop taking notes, unless it is to record an obstacle on which you need to follow up. Minutes from a Daily Scrum are both unnecessary and useless—the Daily Scrum is not where we make decisions; it is where we create the transparency that allows us to make decisions after the Daily Scrum. If the damage is already done, and the dynamics of the meeting are that everyone is speaking directly to the ScrumMaster and not to each other, there is a simple solution. The ScrumMaster should start the Daily Scrum as usual—and then stare at his or her feet. By refusing to make eye contact, the ScrumMaster is basically saying, "look at someone else." This works. When the team member cannot make eye contact with the ScrumMaster, he or she will be forced to make eye contact with someone else on the team, which is exactly what you want. Keep this up for a few days, then start making eye contact again. If all goes well, the new behavior of talking to others on the team will stick. If it does not, and the team starts talking to the ScrumMaster again, start looking at your feet again. It may take a few days, but it will eventually work. Once your team starts using the Daily Scrum meeting for what it was intended, the meeting will increase in value.

4. **Lack of discipline:** Doing the Daily Scrum correctly requires a clear understanding of how the Daily Scrum is supposed to work and what the Daily Scrum is supposed to accomplish (the latter has already been discussed in this section). All Certified ScrumMasters are taught how the Daily Scrum is supposed to work, but many lack the assertiveness to maintain the discipline needed to ensure that the meeting is handled properly. As you may already know, the proper form for the Daily Scrum is to do it at the same time and place every day, to gather the team into a single location, and then for each team member to briefly (but with enough detail to be understandable) answer each of the following questions:
   - What have I done since the previous Daily Scrum?
   - What do I plan to do between now and the next Daily Scrum?
   - What, if anything, is keeping me from getting my work done?

During the course of the meeting, clarifying questions may be asked, but only to ensure understanding of the answers to the questions.

Detailed conversations are to be deferred until after the Daily Scrum is completed, and no one but the team is allowed to speak during the meeting (questions and comments from people outside the team are forbidden). The reasons for these rules are clear. For a Daily Scrum meeting to accomplish its goal of creating transparency across the team preparatory to inspecting the current state of the team and deciding what actions to take next, the team must be able to focus on clearly understanding and interpreting the transparency created by the Daily Scrum. Detailed technical conversations and questions from outside the team interrupt that understanding and result in much less efficient adaptations on the part of the Scrum team. In other words, if the meeting is not allowed to flow as it is supposed to, the risk of not meeting all of the team's goals by the end of the Sprint is increased.

- **Solution:** Retrain the team on how the Daily Scrum is supposed to work. Explain how the questions are to be answered. Stop any detailed conversations before they get started by politely asking the speaker to "wait just a few more minutes until the Daily Scrum is over." Do not allow any outside observers to speak during the Daily Scrum, using the exact same request, "Wait just a few more minutes until the Daily Scrum is over." Do not allow any exceptions to how the meeting is run. Do not allow lateness; follow up with any violators immediately by explaining that the meeting must be attended by everyone, every day. Always start the meeting on time and never start over for stragglers. By consistently and politely setting the tone for the meeting, the team will soon come to respect what the meeting is intended to do and will begin to see the value in holding the meeting and doing it properly.

The Daily Scrum is a crucial part of the Scrum framework. When the meeting is not managed properly, teams can lose sight of the value provided by the meeting and will often ask for the meeting to be held less often or to be discontinued altogether. It is up to the ScrumMaster to diagnose dysfunctional Daily Scrums and make the proper changes.

HOW DO I KEEP TEAM MEMBERS ENGAGED DURING SPRINT PLANNING?

One of the problems facing many Scrum teams today is how to keep team members engaged in Scrum team meetings. I walk into many meetings and see only one or two members of the team really engaged. Everyone else is sitting around, sometimes participating, and sometimes simply doodling on their notepads. So, how do we make sure that everyone on the team is involved, even those who are participating remotely? Here are some tips that I recommend adopting in your Sprint Planning meetings:

1. Turn off the data projectors. Nothing disengages a team member faster than having all of the information displayed for them on the wall. Come on—you have seen it. You walk into a room; one person is typing on his or her laptop. What they are typing (including all of their mistakes) is appearing on the wall. No one is doing anything but watching until the typing is done. You can almost *hear* the wasted minutes ticking away.

2. If your team is big enough, try this:
   a. Review two backlog items with the Product Owner. Ask questions until everyone is ready to create a solution and assign tasks for the item.
   b. Have the team split itself into two subgroups. Each group takes one of the backlog items and goes into a corner of the conference room or team room, works out a solution to the backlog item, and assigns tasks for the solution.
   c. After 20 minutes, the team comes back together and does a quick presentation of solutions and their tasks. Questions can either result in modifications to the solution or changes, additions, or deletions from the task list. Of course, if the team *really* misses the mark with the solution, the exercise can be repeated to create a better solution.
   d. If the team believes it can complete more backlog items, repeat the process. If the team believes their limit is scheduled, you are done.

3. Get yourself lots of Post-it notes, two or three whiteboards, one or two flip charts, and a digital camera. Encourage *lots* of drawings, notes, and concepts. Take pictures when a concept is completed and move on. Limit discussions only to what is being discussed as viable

solutions (in other words, no unnecessary sidebars). Track backlog item risks or problems that cannot be quickly solved and make tasks out of them to mitigate or solve them.

4. If people get into long conversations about "solution A" versus "solution B" that are no longer discussing the merits of the solutions but, rather, have degenerated into repetition or personal jabs, encourage them to choose one solution and move on (but *do not* make the choice for them). Teams *must* learn how to examine problems and make quick decisions.

5. To bring in remote team members, employ telecommunication tools that allow webcams, shared whiteboard spaces, chatting, desktop sharing, and surveys. The more the remote team members can be spoken to, seen, and heard as if they were actually in the room, the less it feels like they are somewhere else.

6. Remove the chairs from the room.

WHAT SHOULD I DO IF MY TEAM IS HIGHLY SPECIALIZED?

A frequent problem with Scrum teams during the early stages of an agile transition is that the uneven distribution of skills usually results in one or more teams in which the number of people on the team might be acceptable, but everybody specializes in something else. I have seen quite a few variations on this theme, but they usually all suffer from the same problem.

For example, in one case, I coached a team of tool developers. They also provided support for the tools. The problem was that the team supported seven or eight different tools, and everyone on the team was an expert in only one or perhaps two of them. The problem, of course, is that, no matter how hard you try to create a collaborative team, there is only one or two who can work on any given backlog item.

In my opinion, you really have four options in a situation such as this. I discuss each of the four, in no particular order.

Option 1: Status Quo. Make no changes to the team, but while they are working on their backlog items, teach them how to improve their coaching skills, their writing and presentation skills, and their verbal communication skills. They should learn how to work with one another and learn how to bridge the gaps between their knowledge bases.

Team members should be encouraged to teach each other during Sprint Planning, backlog grooming, and design meetings during the Sprint. They should challenge one another based on their understandings of each other's tools. This may not seem like much of an option, but consider the business motivation to do otherwise if one or more of the tools that the team supports is to be replaced by a new one. Cross-training becomes less desirable. What would be desirable? That would be a team that is already performing at a high level.

Option 2: Cross-Train. Employ a rule that no one should work on a backlog item by themselves, and that team members should volunteer for items that are not in their area of expertise, knowing that the recognized "expert" will provide coaching and support. While this will result in some short-term decrease in potential velocity, the practice will pay for itself many times over as the team's knowledge base expands and there are increasing options for getting a backlog item done. This practice is not intended to make everyone an expert on everything—that would be expecting too much. The goal, rather, is to give as many people on the team as possible a fundamental understanding of more of the products or components that the team is responsible for such that they could answer basic user questions, provide support on some of the more common cases, and if necessary have at least a beginning understanding of how to diagnose issues should the resident expert not be available.

Option 3: Refactor the Team. In many cases, if too few people on a team have detailed knowledge of a component or a tool, the underlying cause may be a decision made when the teams were created to put some of the expertise on a different team, responsible for different things. In cases such as this, with the expertise existing in the organization but not on the team, you can either "refactor" the teams (move people around to create the right amount of expertise in the right place) or engage in a variation of option 2, with an expert supporting another team's training (i.e., the expert in team B supports the expert in team A to train more of the members in team A).

Refactoring your teams is something that should be done carefully and when justified by the business situation. Changing team membership can be expensive in terms of the facility costs (moving furniture and supplies); productivity costs (delays incurred because of the move as well as having a new member on the team); and personnel costs (dissatisfaction with the move; a sense of feeling like a chess piece moved as management sees fit, which is demotivating). Essentially, you will end up having to weight the benefit of increased expertise in one area against the cost of the impact in other areas.

Option 4: "Mandated" Cross-Training. As a manager, I worked with one group of employees who had worked so long in their specific piece of a larger product that, even though there were over 20 developers, it seemed like the group's ability to get any one backlog item was constrained by the one or two developers actually trained in that area.[3] The entire group was made up of 15 domain owners and 7 other junior developers only trained in one or two of those domains. In fact, at one point, one of the most valuable developers in the group (to me, anyway) was one who had been with the group only 2 or 3 years but had some expertise in several domains of the product. To improve throughput across the team, I set a few new rules in place:

- No domain owner may change code in his or her domain of the product.
- Anyone may work on any portion of the product as long as it is not in their domain and he or she had a domain owner as an advisor during the work.

This, essentially, forced cross-training by making everyone work outside his or her comfort zone while continuing to use the domain owners, the experts, as advisors. The rules also allowed for domain owners to code as well, but on other portions of the product. Of course, in the case of an emergency (critical defect), the proper domain owner led the diagnosis and solution effort.

I kept this policy in place for 12 months, asking the domain owners to keep track of who in the group was skilled enough to work within their domain with little supervision. When there were at least three who could work within the critical domains (the ones that were the focus of the most backlog items), I relaxed the policy and began letting domain owners work on their own domains again. However, I also required that all backlog items be worked on by at least two people (see "Does Swarming on Small Stories Increase or Decrease Productivity?" in Chapter 12).

What you must be careful to consider in this instance is the likely reaction of your team. Are they going to be willing to do what you ask? Will they push back, telling you that it is more work than it is worth to cross-train? Read your team before you take this step; find out how willing they would be to do this. There is a lot of command and control in it unless you can get the team to agree to these steps voluntarily.

In the end, the extent of the specialization of the team has everything to do with the various types of work they are being asked to do. Your success in limiting the specialization will be directly related to how open your employees are to sharing their unique skills and how threatened they feel by no longer having skills that are unique as a result. As a manager, one of the best things you can do with a team in this situation is to work with each individual employee to develop a plan around "where do they go from here." Employees with unique skills *will* feel threatened when asked to share—even when they are unwilling to admit to the fear, it is there. By working with your employees to make the sharing safe, you can improve your team's chances for spreading their skills.

Be careful with this—be patient and be honest. Push change too hard, and you will end up with a unproductive team.

CAN NEW ITEMS BE INTRODUCED DURING THE SPRINT?

According to the Scrum method, once the Sprint has begun, new items cannot be added to the Sprint. This is done to ensure that the Product Owner is thinking things through before the Sprint begins *and* to avoid unnecessary rework and waste caused by changing the Scrum team's Sprint Goals in the middle of the Sprint. Think about it for a second: If the Scrum team knows that the organization or the Product Owner is going to change the Sprint content once the Sprint starts, how much of a commitment are they really going to make during Sprint Planning? It is important that the Scrum team knows that the commitment they make during Sprint Planning is binding on both sides: the team and management.

Having said that, let us talk about some of the misunderstandings that this rule raises. Here are some common misconceptions and the proper way to handle them in a Scrum team:

If the team cannot completely finish a backlog item in a Sprint, there is nothing they can do about it. This is actually wrong (see next section).

In short, backlog items can be functionally sliced into smaller pieces, keeping one functional piece in the current Sprint and putting the remaining functionality back on the Product Backlog. Remember, the restriction is against *adding* new work; this is not adding work, it is removing some.

Even if the Product Owner wants to make changes, he or she will have to wait until the next Sprint. This, of course, depends on the nature of the change. Scrum expects that new requirements and new information will be discovered during the Sprint. Sometimes, those discoveries lead to minor modifications to what the team is building (a change to how a screen is built or how data are stored). Sometimes, those changes are extensive. If the change does not threaten the commitment that the team has made with the Product Owner, there is no problem. If, however, the newly identified information cannot be added to the Sprint without overloading the Scrum team, the Product Owner's best move is to create a new backlog item with the new information and allow the team to work on it in a future Sprint.

There is one scenario for which the Product Owner can change what the team is working on during the Sprint (sort of). This scenario assumes that the changes that the Product Owner has are so far reaching that the Sprint Goals the Scrum teams have committed to are no longer valid or valuable. In this case, the Product Owner may resort to a Sprint Termination.

A Sprint Termination is an abnormal ending of a Sprint when the Scrum team (including the Product Owner) determines that the Sprint Goals of the Sprint are no longer valuable or attainable. When a termination is declared, work stops, and the team immediately moves to Sprint Review and then to Sprint Retrospective. The goals of these meetings are the same as usual, although they will likely focus on the result of the termination of the Sprint. Then, a new Sprint is planned with the new content and new priorities.

However, a Sprint Termination is not to be used routinely. A termination is expensive, as the team will end up bringing work into the next Sprint to clean up whatever was half done from the previous Sprint.

Therefore, once a Sprint begins, it is generally accepted that the content of the Sprint cannot and should not be modified. Small changes to committed backlog items might be acceptable if they require little effort. Larger changes should be written as new backlog items and deferred until a future Sprint. New backlog items may not be added to the Sprint. One more tip: If you find yourself frequently in the dilemma of identifying important changes but have to wait too long to get the new information into a Sprint, shorten your Sprint length.

HOW DO I HANDLE STORIES THAT ARE STARTED BUT CANNOT BE FINISHED IN A SPRINT?

In many cases, the features that are built by development teams take considerably longer than the length of the iterations in which they are built. This is a common occurrence. Sprints are not timed for the amount of effort that an individual backlog item is going to take. The Sprint ends on the date it is supposed to end, leaving some work unfinished and, in many cases, some work not even started. We mitigate this problem by slicing the features we are building into increasingly smaller pieces of functionality (see backlog grooming, Chapter 4). Smaller backlog items fit better into a Sprint than larger ones. When I teach my classes, I often use the example of ice in a glass. When one fills a glass with large ice cubes (see Figure 13.2), several gaps between the ice cubes can be seen in the glass. However, when we break the ice into much smaller pieces, the same ice (and often more) fits into the glass, filling in all of the gaps previously seen (see Figure 13.3).

FIGURE 13.2
Glass containing large ice cubes. Note empty space among the cubes.

FIGURE 13.3
Glass containing crushed ice. Note little to no space among the cubes.

On the surface this comparison suffices, but as we look more closely at the user stories in question, they are not so easily sliced as simply crushing ice cubes. User stories are intended to represent or describe customer-valued functionality. So, when we slice them to allow them to fit more easily into a Sprint, we must be careful how we do it.

For example, take a familiar user story:

As a User, I Want a Simple Sign-in Screen So I Can Identify Myself Before I Start Using the Application.

There are right ways and wrong ways to slice the story in the title into smaller pieces. Let us look at the wrong way by slicing this user story into a series of steps:

- Design the sign-in screen.
- Build the sign-in screen.
- Write the code behind the screen that validates the user ID and password.
- Test the sign-in screen.
- Update the database specification.
- Write the functional specifications.

So, why are these stories wrong? Better yet, what is wrong with them? First, from a purely structural standpoint, a user story that says, "Write the code behind the screen that validates the user ID and password" is not going to be valued highly by a customer. In other words, few customers appreciate, much less care, that a specific piece of coding has been completed, particularly if there is nothing for them to see. Imagine that demonstration: "Well, no, Mr. Customer, you can't actually see it working yet. The code works, but the screen isn't set up. Sorry."

More important, when a Scrum team finishes a user story and they say that they are DONE with it, as a Product Owner, you want there to be a clear understanding of what DONE means, and you want to be able to see some kind of working functionality that can be demonstrated, discussed, and even improved. The user story, "Update the database specification," cannot be demonstrated or discussed. While the developer can say, "Yes, the database specification has been updated," being DONE with the database specification does not tell you if the database has been updated, how close the team is to actually being DONE with the sign-in screen feature, and if the specification changes were the right ones.

Let us slice our original user story again but from a functional perspective. Here are some better slices of the original user story:

- Create a sign-in screen that does not collect any data but provides application access.
- Add the ability to enter a username and password.
- Add error handling for when the password is entered wrong once.
- Add error handling for when the password is entered wrong twice.
- Add error handling for when the password is entered wrong a third time.

Obviously, there are several more scenarios we could add to this list, but these are enough to make the point. As you look at each story, you can see how each story ends with something that can be demonstrated. In addition, there is no ambiguity with regard to being DONE with a story. When a team says that they are done building the story, "Add the ability to add a username and password," it is clear that the Product Owner should be able to look at the log-in screen now and see spaces for the username and the password. Furthermore, the Product Owner understands that the team is saying, "Whatever you see there is what we believe is what you wanted; we're done with it."

Having said all this, let us now answer the original question, "How do I handle stories that are started but cannot be finished in a Sprint?" As I said in the beginning of this section, it is common that you will be partially finished with a backlog item when the Sprint ends because Sprints are not set up to correspond with the anticipated duration of the backlog items in the Sprint.

So, when you are stuck with a partially completed story at the end of a Sprint, here is what your options are:

- Do nothing. Let the Sprint end and return the story and all incomplete tasks to the Release Backlog (or Product Backlog) for a future Sprint. While the likelihood is high that you will just bring the story and the tasks back into the next Sprint, it is not a guarantee, so put the story and tasks back into the Product Backlog and go from there.
- Before the end of the Sprint, see if you can slice the user story you are working on into a piece that you *can* finish before the Sprint ends. Reestimate the part of the story that you are doing so that it properly reflects what was actually completed (the team should have a velocity that actually reflects their accomplishments). Finish the story you can finish and put the newly sliced piece of the story into the Product Backlog. Here is an example of what I mean: Say, for example, you are working on the user story that adds the username and the password to the log-in screen when you discover you are not going to be able to finish. You can slice this story into two smaller stories, one that only adds the username to the log-in screen and one that adds the password to the log-in screen. Put the "password story" into the Product Backlog and attempt to finish the username piece of the story during the current Sprint.

That is pretty much it. There are no other allowable options. You may not add days to the Sprint to finish the story—that is definitely *not allowed* in Scrum.

HOW SHOULD I HANDLE URGENT REQUESTS IN THE MIDDLE OF A SPRINT?

Urgent requests, like changes in requirements or critical defects, are a fact of life in software engineering. They are difficult to predict and frequently need to be addressed on a case-by-case basis against the goals already set by the Scrum team. While it is far more efficient to keep the Scrum team focused on the goals set during Sprint Planning, there are still conventions in the framework to handle the last-second requirement change or the critical defect.

Having allowed for the critical defect or urgent requirement, one should first consider: Is it worth interrupting my Scrum team (or teams) to deal with this late change? Is the defect or requirements truly so important that it cannot wait until the next iteration? While this seems like an obvious question, if you are new to agile development, your primary experience with project management is probably with a waterfall project, during which there is, by definition, *no good time* when you can change the plans of your teams. However, with Scrum, good times to change your team's plans happen at the end of every Sprint. With Sprints so short, the question you are really asking yourself now is, "Can this defect wait 3 weeks until the beginning of the next Sprint?" or "Can this new requirement be built in 2 more weeks when the next Sprint begins?" If the answer is, "Yes, it can wait," you have just saved yourself a lot of frustration. Just add the defect or new requirement to the Product Backlog, and your Scrum team will take care of the rest—it really is that simple.

However, allowing for the answer to be, "No, it really needs to get done right now," we do have options.

Option 1: Direct Insertion. Scrum really does not allow for the insertion of any new work into the Sprint except for critical defects. However, I tend to allow some balancing for minor changes in the Sprint by involving the entire team and considering the size of the change, whether something else can be removed that the team has not started. In other words, if we can make the change without significant impact, we can consider a change to the Sprint goals. To do this, get the ScrumMaster and Product Owner together with the rest of the team and explain what needs to be added to their Sprint Goals and why it is so important (you really do need to explain why; if you do not, or you cannot, the team may think that you are subverting the Scrum framework and the Product Owner's authority). Let the team ask questions and, once they are done, they will decide how to incorporate the work, how to reorganize around the change and what, if anything, needs to be removed from the Sprint to have an achievable Sprint Backlog. In some cases, the team may have already made someone responsible for defects; in this case, inserting the defect into the Sprint is much easier as it only involves that individual. Whatever changes to the Sprint Goals need to be made as a result are then handled by the team member responsible for defects working with the rest of the team. If the impact, however, is significant, the second option should be used.

Option 2: Sprint Termination. Scrum also allows for the complete termination of the Sprint should the team (including the Product Owner) or management decide that the Sprint Goals are, for the most part, no longer achievable or no longer desirable in the currently planned Sprint. To do this, you will need to meet with the entire team and discuss what you need added and why (yes, this is a lot like the previous option). The team will ask questions to better understand the change. If they then decide that, with the change incorporated into the Sprint, there is no way to achieve the majority of the Sprint Goals, they will terminate the Sprint. When this happens, they will hold a Sprint Review to discuss with the Product Owner what was finished during the Sprint; then they will hold a Sprint Retrospective meeting to discuss what happened (including the circumstances leading up to the decision to terminate); finally, they will hold a Sprint Planning meeting to replan a new Sprint that includes the change that needed to be introduced.

Other than these two options, there are no other allowable methods for introducing new content into a Sprint. Since the Sprint Goals represent a negotiated commitment between the developers and the Product Owner, it is important for the purposes of efficiency, not to mention trust and self-management, to honor the commitment and allow changes to it only through ongoing negotiation between the developers and the Product Owner.

Also, consider that, if there is a consistent flow of high-priority changes to Sprints that are already under way, you may want to shorten your Sprint length.

HOW SHOULD I HANDLE A SICK OR OTHERWISE ABSENT TEAM MEMBER?

Handling a sick or absent (we will just go with "absent" in this section) team member depends on a number of factors, not the least of which include (a)

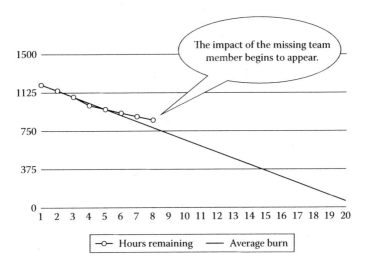

FIGURE 13.4

Sprint Burndown showing a diminished daily velocity,

the role the individual plays on the team, (b) the length of the absence, (c) whether the absence was planned or unplanned, and (d) whether the individual was there for Sprint Planning.

If the absent team member is a junior programmer who does not play a significant role in the direction of the team, the impact to the team will be considerably less than if the absent team member is the team's central repository of experience and knowledge. The length of the absence also plays a major factor in how the team responds.

Some absences are planned; vacations and scheduled training can be taken into account during Sprint Planning and the impact of the absence directly factored into the team's commitment to the Product Owner. But, of course, many absences are not only unplanned, but also occur after Sprint Planning, when the Sprint Goals cannot reflect the impact of the absence.

In the end, all of this comes down to the team's ability to self-manage their workload (something that is, according to Scrum, their responsibility to do). Unplanned absences result in projections and commitments that cannot be sustained when the team actually begins to deal with the absence. For example, in Figure 13.4, the team has committed to 1,200 hours of work, only to discover 8 days into the 4-week Sprint that their commitment is becoming increasingly unachievable. Daily examination of the Sprint Burndown chart (part of the team's responsibilities during the Sprint) will allow the team to see the nature of the impact that the absent team member is having on the team's performance against their commitment.

When the burndown shows that the commitment cannot be achieved, the team is expected to respond by working with the Product Owner to modify their commitment and make it achievable again.

HOW CAN SCRUM BE APPLIED IN A TEST TEAM?

The question of applying Scrum in a test team is really a question of compromising Scrum (and the final quality of your application). The reason I say this is that having a "test team" means that your organization has already made the decision to have a separate team do "testing." Now, this may mean that the "development teams" are doing some testing and the "test teams" are doing more testing—that would be a reasonable implementation of Scrum. However, if your organization has created the situation in which one Scrum team writes the software and another Scrum team tests the software, you need to stop what you are doing and seriously consider how you are implementing agile development. Scrum teams that can write software and then hand that software over to someone else to make sure it is right are Scrum teams that will always write poor-quality software.

If you are suggesting the former scenario, in which the test Scrum teams supplement the work of the development Scrum teams, read on.

If you must have a Scrum test team (which happens frequently when the product does not have sufficient automated testing), your test team will operate similarly to your Scrum teams. The teams will probably have a Sprint length the same as the development teams. The test teams will do Sprint Planning in which they will review what they plan to test. Test teams do Daily Scrums at which they discuss their current situation and plan what, if anything, to do differently. Test teams do Sprint Reviews in which they review what they completed during the Sprint, and Sprint Retrospectives to search for better ways to do their jobs.

There are, fundamentally, two different ways to engage your test teams with your development teams. The first and simplest way is to put the test team in "lockstep" with the development teams. In other words, what the development teams finish in Sprint 1, the test teams test in Sprint 2. What the development teams finish in Sprint 2, the test teams test in Sprint 3, and so on. This can be an effective manner for getting the testing work done, particularly for an organization with little-to-no test infrastructure. The downside is that the development team will keep getting interrupted in Sprint 3 to fix defects created in Sprint 2.

The second configuration interleaves the development and the testing in a more iterative and backlog-item-based implementation. In this configuration, as the development team finishes a backlog item (the Product Owner might do a preliminary review and approval of the item during the Sprint), the item is passed directly to the test team; the test team then tests the item, starting the work as soon as possible. The advantage to this configuration is reduced risk and backlog item cycle time during the Sprint because defects are found sooner and fixed earlier. Defects that are found quickly and fixed quickly are less expensive to fix because the mind of the developer is often not so far removed from the code where the defect was found.

The second configuration is a little more complex, unfortunately, because of the nature of the workflow from the development team. What I mean by this is, while the development team can plan an entire Sprint from the content of the Product Backlog, the test team cannot plan to work on something until it actually is finished by the development team and is ready for the test team. A test team cannot easily hold a Sprint Planning meeting for an entire 3- or 4-week Sprint because there is simply no way to predict when or how much of the work will actually be completed by the development team. For this reason, it is common for the test teams to accumulate completed items from the development teams during 1 week and then plan and execute a 1-week Sprint during the following week, when the accumulated items are then tested.

HOW DOES SYSTEM TESTING FIT IN SCRUM?

In agile development, all testing is done as a continuously repeating check of the functioning system. In today's technology, it is similar to the continuous monitoring of many computer-enhanced automobiles, which continually check the functioning of the automobile and alert the driver when there is a potential problem with the oil, the water, the engine emissions, the engine safety systems, the engine temperature, the tire pressure, the fuel injector, and many other interesting items, depending on the sensors built into the automobile.

The software that we write today is complex. Thousands of functions, third-party interfaces, various operating systems, different client environments, millions of possible decisions, and an endless supply of surprises in data we have not experienced create a situation that quickly exceeds the ability of our developers to predict outcomes. Combine that with multiple releases of software and highly configurable software that require the ability to verify the actions of all of the valid and invalid combinations of configurations and you quickly realize that you are building software you cannot possibly completely test, much less test it when you are finished writing it.

Agile development suggests that software should be tested while it is being built. A good Scrum team writes automated unit, acceptance, and workflow tests as they actually build the functions that they are planning to test. An XP practice, test-driven development, even builds the unit test at the same time as the actual code is written, ensuring that the code is properly and completely tested at every stage of development. As the Scrum team builds the code and the tests, an hourly automated build verifies that what it just wrote did not introduce any defects. Every evening, a nightly build actually rebuilds and reruns every automated test that exists to that point to ensure that everything still works. Some organizations actually run the "nightly" type of build on a continuous basis during the day, alongside the hourly builds, just to get faster feedback or if the rebuild of the entire product is starting to take longer than 12–14 hours.

System testing (validating the overall operation of the entire product installed in a "production-like" environment) should be done just like the nightly builds, with a new version of the product installed in an environment similar or identical to a production environment. In a purely agile environment, the nightly build *is* the system test; the rebuilt product is installed in a production-like environment and completely tested by executing all of the currently existing automated tests. Unfortunately, most organizations cannot create this type of workflow for a variety of reasons. Here are some of the ways organizations "gracefully downgrade" to "less-agile" forms of system testing:

- Because the system test environment also doubles as a demo environment, the people using it as a demo environment do not want it rebuilt continuously. In these instances, the system test is often done based on the calendar (only on Fridays, only during the first weekend of the month, only after the end of a Sprint). In these instances, the system test is run only a few times per iteration (or less). This can create a problem as it may allow a defect to go unnoticed for weeks. The solution is to spend the money to create a system test environment. I know it sounds expensive, but your developers cost more when they have to fix defects weeks after the defects were created.

- Because the nightly build takes too long, the system test environment is only refreshed and tested when the nightly build is successful. This situation is not too bad—as the system test is run increasingly when the quality of the nightly build improves. Chances are that if your nightly build and test failed, your system test would also have failed. However, because the build takes too long, the window for defects is opened more broadly. The solution is to devote some time to shortening your product build time. There are many ways to multithread and distribute the compiles so that the overall build time can be remarkably reduced (I worked at one organization where the nightly compiles were distributed across the developers' desktops; this was a fantastic use of a resource that was not in use that time of night).

- Because the product installation is not automated, the system test is only done once a Sprint using the most recent successful nightly build. Many organizations forget to automate their product installation scripts. I believe this problem will be greatly reduced in the future as there is more and more pressure to automate installs and upgrades, but the problem is alive and well today and is one of the more common reasons why defects get into the product and are not found for weeks. The solution is to automate your product installation (there are many software packages available today to help with this). By the way, do not forget to automate your database installation and upgrade scripting.

- Because none of the system tests are automated, the system test is either done by a separate testing team on a continuous basis, *or* the system test is done only at the end of the project, which is not good. When system testing is delayed until the end of the project, you will experience a potentially long "integration phase"; your Scrum teams will have to build, test, fix, build, test, fix, build, test, fix—on and on until all of the defects they should have caught during the earlier Sprints go away. This condition is the antithesis to agile testing. This is like having a warning light on the dashboard of your automobile that, when it lights up, it means that your engine now needs so much repair that you might as well buy another car. While organizations usually blame this on a lack of resources, that is really only half the truth. The situation was caused by bad planning; it persists because of the lack of resources. The solution is to start automating your testing with any new or changed functionality. Create coverage tests over the rest of the application so you can at least see when critical functions or features misbehave. Automate your build processes and automate your installation scripts as soon as possible. In the meantime, you might want to try a staggered development-test pattern by which, for example, you develop for two or three Sprints and then hold a short Sprint when the product is retested. Then, develop for a few more Sprints and hold another short Sprint for testing. While this would seem to extend the development schedule, the reality is that your teams will find more defects faster if they interleave the testing with the development. Try to do all of the testing at the end, and you are actually creating the worst condition for your teams to find and fix defects.

REFERENCE

Schiel, James A. 2010. *Enterprise-Scale Agile Software Development.* Boca Raton, FL: CRC Press.

ENDNOTES

1. The entire body of knowledge of Scrum can be found in the Scrum Guide at http://www.scrum.org/scrumguides
2. ScrumWorks is still going strong with its current owner, CollabNet.
3. This example is actually about a large group of developers, but the same concept can work with a Scrum team (or even multiple related Scrum teams).

14

Agile Product Management

WHAT IS THE RELEASE BACKLOG?

Technically, in Scrum, there is no such thing as a Release Backlog. Scrum defines only a single Product Backlog containing everything that the Product Owner wants to "do" to the product. However, many coaches (myself included) talk about the *Release Backlog* in terms of that portion of the Product Backlog targeted for inclusion in the current release of our product. In that sense, the Release Backlog becomes the top of the Product Backlog (Figure 14.1).

Another view of the Release Backlog has it as a completely separate list from the Product Backlog. In this arrangement, the Product Backlog is still a list of everything that Product Owner wants to do to the product until a backlog item is specifically allocated to a release. Then, the backlog item is moved from the Product Backlog to the proper Release Backlog. Several Release Backlogs could be maintained at the same time, allowing for the building of one release, while simultaneously planning multiple future releases (Figure 14.2).

The presence of an item on the Release Backlog is not a commitment for inclusion in the backlog. Like the Product Backlog, the Release Backlog does not include dates or timeframes; it is no more than a list being completed at the pace and quality made possible by the Scrum teams. Of course, backlog items can be moved from one Release Backlog to another as needed.

HOW DO I DETERMINE PROJECT BUDGET FROM A PRODUCT BACKLOG?

In an environment in which "big design up front" is not allowed and requirements are progressively elaborated, creating a project budget can be a bit of

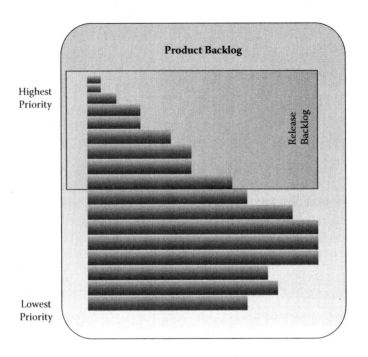

FIGURE 14.1
Relationship between Product Backlog and Release Backlog consisting of highest priority elements.

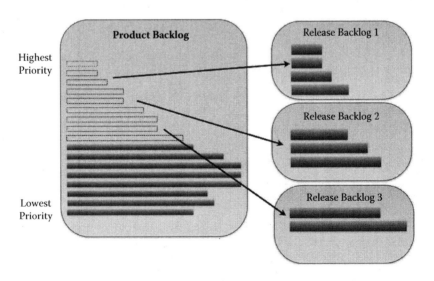

FIGURE 14.2
Relationship between Product Backlog and Release Backlog consisting of buckets of upcoming releases. Backlog items are dropped into buckets when they are slated for a specific release.

a challenge. In the traditional project, and particularly in the case of the development organization trying to create a fixed-price/fixed-scope agreement, knowing what you are going to build and how you are going to build it is a prerequisite to starting the project. On the surface, agile development seems to lack the ability to satisfy this fundamental need.

In reality, the difficulty that we perceive in this situation is just that, a perception. The reality is that, even when we estimate the items we are going to build, add in various time-consuming factors (including discovery of new requirements during the project), and then pad it some more, our final estimate for the project is partly influenced by the scope of what we are planning to build and heavily driven by our assumptions of the unknowns that will surface during the project.

Employing some of the same principles used in conventional techniques, but with an eye toward statistical probability, lean development techniques, and the fundamental understanding that software requirements seldom reveal themselves until after we start developing, we can accomplish project budgeting without committing ourselves to a lengthy and costly up-front effort. Here is how it works:

The basic concept behind story point estimation is that every feature that we, as application developers, build is to a large extent affected by the same unknown elements. That is, as we build a feature, there will be some number of unknown factors that will affect the overall effort required to complete the feature; every feature, relative to its size, will suffer unknown factors to a proportionate degree. Large features will experience substantial unknown factors; small features will experience much less. When a large enough population of features is estimated, the differences begin to approach an average (usually "a large-enough population" is more than 30 features, a threshold easily attained in most projects).

Story point estimation takes advantage of this by simplifying the task of estimation. Instead of trying to figure out what a requirement means *and* trying to determine a solution for the requirement *and* trying to determine how to build the solution *and* trying to add motivations into our solution to account for the unexpected—instead of all that, story point estimation simply suggests that features that seem similar in complexity, size, and risk should likewise have the same story point size assigned. Features that, therefore, have the same story point assignment will also take a similar amount of time to complete. In this way, we no longer have to know how much effort is entailed in a 2-point story; we simply need to understand how many points a team can finish in a given iteration.

Velocity-Based Commitments

To create a project budget, we have two choices, each of which are, to a large degree, mutually exclusive. First, if our agile development teams are already formed and have a number of successful iterations behind them, we can assume that we know, or are reasonably certain of, their velocity (how many points of work they can complete in an iteration). Let us assume that we have five Scrum teams, each of which has a measurable velocity. We can track velocity on a bar chart like in Figure 14.3.

There is some variability in the velocities attained each Sprint, of course, but even that can be factored into the understanding of the team's velocity in terms of confidence ranges if necessary (i.e., team A has an average velocity of 35 points ± 15%). To determine the velocity of our "development system," we simply add the velocities of our teams together (of course, factoring in that confidence range as well, if desired). When we determine our system velocity (generally a moving average of the previously completed three iterations) based on the values shown in Figure 14.3, we might determine our system velocity to be 150 points.

Let us further assume that our Scrum teams, following the proper practice of Scrum and backlog grooming, have estimated everything on the backlog for the next project. If, for example, that estimate works out to

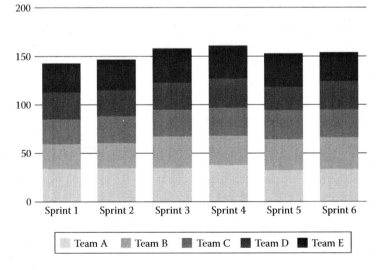

FIGURE 14.3

Combined velocities (points per Sprint) of several Scrum teams during a release. As long as you do not try to compare velocities across teams and the teams remain consistent in their estimates, this type of chart can show relative changes in system velocity.

a total of 1,500 points, we can assume that our next project will require approximately 10 iterations to complete (the total backlog size 1,500 points divided by our system velocity 150 points). Now that you have the number of iterations, you can create your budget from the cost of your teams over that period of time.

The drawbacks to this method are many:

- You must already have teams formed and working long enough to establish a demonstrable velocity.
- The project that you are estimating must be somewhat similar to the projects your teams are already working on in terms of tool kit, risk, and skill set.
- You should not be making or planning to make any substantial change to team membership.

T-Shirt Sizing

The other method for creating a project budget uses the concepts of story point estimation combined with more traditional methods. In T-shirt, we do story point estimation, but on larger stories and with less granularity in our estimate sizes. In other words, the typical Scrum team (assuming that they are using a Fibonacci sequence for their story points) works on stories that are 1, 2, and 3 points and estimates larger stories, usually using 5, 8, 13, 21, 34, and 55 (there are many different numbering schemes and approaches in use; your experience may vary). However, when we do story point sizes, the sizes we use are

- XS (extra small)
- S (small)
- M (medium)
- L (large)
- XL (extra large)

In general, XS ends up being stories that would fit into the Sprint; all other sizes are bigger. The estimation process remains the same—comparing stories to those already estimated, making the decision whether a story is bigger or smaller than other similar stories, and estimating them appropriately. T-shirt sizing is the first step in the budgeting process.

When finished with T-shirt sizing, you should then take all of the stories in a single size and review your decisions. Since you are creating the baseline (e.g., what a small story is) in an ad hoc manner, you may discover some "drifting"; your idea of a particular size may have started from one perspective but slowly changed into something smaller or larger. By reviewing each story within each size, you can capture some that, on second glance, need to be moved up or down to the next T-shirt size.

After the review, you will then take a sample of five or six stories from each T-shirt size. One at a time, estimate the stories in person-days, person-weeks, or man-months—whatever is the norm in your organization. If all of the stories within a single T-shirt size end up being fairly similar, you can use the average of the samples to create a rough cost equivalent for each story. If the sample does not produce a consistent average, estimate a few more stories until you get a consistent result (you might also want to consider whether some of the stories in the sample are in the wrong size categorization). If you discover that your XS stories are all fairly close to an average of 12 person-days and if there are 20 stories, the total size of your XS stories is 20 × 12, or 240 person-days. The total estimate of your project is the total of the averages of each T-shirt size (Schiel 2010, 198–203).

HOW DO YOU BALANCE CUSTOMER REQUIREMENTS AGAINST TECHNICAL REQUIREMENTS?

The typical Product Owner is going to be focused on customer-facing features much more than any requests to refactor a module or redesign a component. In fact, included with the responsibilities of the Product Owner is the need to maximize return on investment (ROI; measured as the value of the backlog item over the cost of the backlog item).

Table 14.1 shows a simple Product Backlog in which each of the items has an effort estimation provided in story points by the Scrum team and a value estimation provided on a scale of 0–10 by the Product Owner.

Our sample Product Backlog contains backlog items that provide functionality ("I want to admit a student"), provide scalability ("I want 50 students … ") and provide infrastructure reinvestment ("We need to upgrade … "). A typical backlog will provide many examples of all three types of items: functions, nonfunctional requirements, and infrastructure.

TABLE 14.1

A Simple Product Backlog

No.	Item	Effort (SP)	Value
1	I want to admit a student.	100	8
2	I want to log on to the system.	20	2
3	I want to register a student for a class.	60	8
4	We need to upgrade the database to add new tables.	75	1
5	I want to create a class.	60	6
6	I want the registration to fail if the class is full.	12	2
7	We need to refactor the student module to support enrollment in multiple classes.	40	3
8	I want 50 students to be able to register for the same class at the same time.	80	3

SP, story points.

So, our Product Owner, Paul, who recently learned Scrum and knows that he needs to maximize ROI, creates spreadsheet formulas that automatically sort his backlog based on maximum value over minimum cost. The result, after his work is the backlog shown in Table 14.2.

Figure 14.2 shows the backlog from Table 14.1 sorted in descending ROI order. The ROI was calculated as *Value/Effort* (SP).

This arrangement of the backlog mathematically maximizes the ROI of the product. Unfortunately, it misses the fact that there are some backlog items that must come before other items. This is known as the item

TABLE 14.2

The Sorted Product Backlog

No.	Item	Effort (SP)	Value
6	I want the registration to fail if the class is full.	12	2
3	I want to register a student for a class.	60	8
2	I want to log on to the system.	20	2
5	I want to create a class.	60	6
1	I want to admit a student.	100	8
7	We need to refactor the student module to support enrollment in multiple classes.	40	3
8	I want 50 students to be able to register for the same class at the same time.	80	3
4	We need to upgrade the database to add new tables.	75	1

SP, story points.

sequence (as opposed to its *priority*). To understand the issue, look at the backlog in Table 14.2; how would we complete a registration without a student (admitted in item 1) or a class (created in item 5)?

More important, notice the items at the bottom of Paul's list: a refactoring item (item 7), a scalability item (item 8), and an infrastructure item (item 4), there because Paul has placed such a low value on these items ("After all," he said, "the customer isn't going to care if we do them").

Many Product Owners feel the same way. Their focus is on satisfying the customer and maximizing value. Many Product Owners, not having come from a product development background, do not always understand the continuous reinvestment in product code that comes with writing a product. Consider this: Companies that develop and sell software often talk about the advantages of their product in terms of total cost of ownership (TCO). But, how many times do you hear anybody talking about the "total cost of code ownership" (TCCO[1])?

TCCO is about the cost of every line of code that your Scrum teams write when building a product. These costs would be the responsibility of the organization that wrote the code and mostly reoccur every time changes are made to the product. Ignoring the relatively minor costs of storage and archiving, some of the costs of code ownership are

1. Planning and writing the code
2. Documenting the code
3. Maintaining the documentation
4. Writing the tests to verify the code
5. Fixing defects in the code that occur initially and afterward when the code changes
6. Refactoring the code as new features are added
7. Upgrading or maintaining the services, systems, or packages required by the code

Product Owners are not focused on TCCO; they are focused on customer-facing functionality. The problem we face in Scrum teams is figuring out how to get our Product Owners to understand that the costs of code ownership must be dealt with in much the same way we deal with customer-facing functionality. In my experience, there seem to be two approaches to this problem and they can be used separately or, in many cases, together.

Approach 1: Tax the Functionality

Have you ever rented a car, thrilled with the "low, low daily rate" of $24.99, just to discover, when you return the car, that the rate is closer to $67 a day? In a large part, that considerable increase in the rate is the insurance. But, the rest of the daily rate (above and beyond the $24.99) is taxes and charges. Now, why are they there? Of course, the taxes and charges are there, essentially, to pay for government-related services that make it possible to rent cars in the first place.

A lot of Scrum teams do the same thing when they estimate backlog items. If a particular customer requires a redesign of a module for the feature to be properly built, the customer includes the redesign in with the cost of the feature. If a backlog item requires changes to a piece of code that is not yet covered by unit tests and the organization has a policy to cover all new and changed code with unit tests, the team will include the cost of the tests with the effort to build the feature.

Sometimes this approach works well, and sometimes it does not. And sometimes, it is seen by the Product Owners as a dishonest way of getting work done without having to create new backlog items (for those of you with political acumen in the United States, this is similar to the "pork" our congressmen and senators often attach to bills, like building an airport on an Alaskan island that is only sparsely inhabited only part of the year). Clearly, you have to be as up front with your "taxes" as the rental car agency is.

Approach 2: Build Infrastructure into the Backlog

In the CSM training I provide, one of the slides talks about the content of the backlog in terms of the types of items that you might find on the backlog. In class, we talk about how Scrum defines the content of the backlog as containing features, defects, and infrastructure items. As we discussed with Paul's backlog, the problem with putting the infrastructure on the backlog is that the Product Owner often cannot see the benefit of the infrastructure,

So, we have to create a method of valuation that puts the customer-facing feature and the product-facing infrastructure on the same level. We can do this by adding another level of valuation to our backlogs. In the initial example, there were two values assigned to each backlog item: effort and value. To balance the features against the infrastructure, we will go with three values for each backlog item: effort, benefit, and penalty. They work like this:

- **Effort** is unchanged. It is a measure of the rough cost (in human resources) to build the backlog item.
- **Benefit** is a new piece of the value of the backlog item. Benefit is usually a 0–10 measure of how much value the customer places on the backlog item. A 0 would indicate a backlog item that customers give no value. A 10 would indicate an extremely valuable item for customers.
- **Penalty** is the second new piece of the value of the backlog item. Penalty is usually a 0–10 measure of how much the product is affected if the backlog item is *not* done. A 0 would indicate a backlog item that would not have a negative effect on the product if it were not built. A 10 would indicate a backlog item that, if not done, would cause the product to be unusable. So, for example,
  - Adding a new feature to the product would likely have a value of 0. If the feature is not built, the product still works.
  - Upgrading to a new version of a database manager because the warranty for the old one is about to expire would likely have a high penalty value, perhaps 8 or 10. If we do not complete the upgrade, the product might be unusable (or at least not cost effective) using an out-of-warranty version of the database management system (DBMS).
  - Adding functionality that improves scalability or performance would likely have a penalty anywhere between 2 and 10, depending on the necessary capabilities of the product against its current capabilities.

Let us go back to the original backlog and add a penalty factor. Table 14.3 shows the backlog from Table 14.1 with value now represented as a combination of benefit (on a scale of 0–10) and penalty (on a scale of 0–10).

With the "value" of a backlog item now split into benefit and penalty, we can re-sort the backlog. In doing so, we get the prioritization in Table 14.4, which shows the backlog from Table 14.3 sorted by a new ROI. The new ROI is calculated as (Benefit + Penalty)/Effort. The addition of penalty to the value calculation helps us to level the playing field across customer-facing features and infrastructure needs.

This new prioritization gives us a slightly different backlog. There are still problems with it, however. No form of automated prioritization is

TABLE 14.3

The Product Backlog

No.	Item	Effort (SP)	Benefit	Penalty
1	I want to admit a student.	100	8	0
2	I want to log on to the system.	20	2	0
3	I want to register a student for a class.	60	8	0
4	We need to upgrade the database to add new tables.	75	1	9
5	I want to create a class.	60	6	0
6	I want the registration to fail if the class is full.	12	2	0
7	We need to refactor the student module to support enrollment in multiple classes.	40	3	6
8	I want 50 students to be able to register for the same class at the same time.	80	3	3

SP, story points.

going to get you exactly what you want. As you can see in this backlog, sequencing of items is still a problem. For example, it is going to be difficult to cause a registration to fail because of a full class if we have not yet figured out how to build a class (item 5) or register a student (item 1).

TABLE 14.4

The Product Backlog Sorted by Benefit and Penalty

No.	Item	Effort (SP)	Benefit	Penalty
7	We need to refactor the student module to support enrollment in multiple classes.	40	3	6
6	I want the registration to fail if the class is full.	12	2	0
3	I want to register a student for a class.	60	8	0
4	We need to upgrade the database to add new tables.	75	1	9
2	I want to log on to the system.	20	2	0
5	I want to create a class.	60	6	0
1	I want to admit a student.	100	8	0
8	I want 50 students to be able to register for the same class at the same time.	80	3	3

SP, story points.

However, as you can see in the latest version of the backlog, defining value as a function of benefit and penalty can help your Product Owner prioritize from a slightly more level playing field.

Of course, the next challenge is going to be getting your developers to talk about infrastructure changes (refactoring a class, redesigning a component) in terms of the consequences of not doing it. In my experience, developers will find it easier to do this than trying to sell infrastructure changes on their merit.

HOW DO YOU FORECAST COMPLETION IN A BACKLOG FILLED WITH EPICS?

Let us be honest—the question of how you forecast completion in a backlog filled with epics could just as easily be rephrased: How do you forecast completion with a waterfall project schedule that seems to be exact, but really is not?

Or, how about this as a question: If I cannot accurately forecast completion after having spent thousands of hours and tens of thousands of dollars creating a project schedule, what am I supposed to do?

I am not a waterfall-basher; I will be among the first people to tell you that there are projects that work well with waterfall projects. I have run several of those projects myself, so I feel somewhat qualified to identify them when they come around.

However, the fundamental problem that the question of this section poses is, how do I accurately forecast completion when software development is so unpredictable? Realistically, *that* is actually the problem here—not agile, not user stories. Software development is an unpredictable exercise (Schiel 2010, 299–301). It is extremely complex and, as I tell many of my students, one of the few engineering practices for which we create something from nothing but the ideas in our heads.

In agile development, we recognize that we *can* create a rough approximation of what we have yet to build (e.g., approximately 20 man-months). We can temper that approximation by adding a margin of error so that we are actually providing a range of probability (e.g., approximately 20 man-months ± 15%). We can also leverage the properties of random distribution and statistical analysis to put some real science behind our approximations (which allows us to use the values more effectively). What agile development provides that waterfall does not is the realization that a systematically determined rough approximation is worth as much as an expensive project schedule in forecasting completion.

We of course need to start with a fully estimated backlog (see "How Do I Determine Project Budget from a Product Backlog?" in this chapter for more information). It is important to understand that any effective agile estimation scheme is going to recognize that the larger the backlog item is, the larger the margin of error will be. For that reason, estimation schemes tend to provide allowable values (usually doubling or Fibonacci sequences) that become increasingly less precise as they get larger. For example, for very large backlog items, teams using a Fibonacci sequence will tend to want to use values like 13, 21, 34, 55, and 89. When estimating large items, teams will have to choose between a number that feels too small and a number that feels equally too big; as teams tend to be conservative, they will often assign the higher value. However, given that those same teams tend to overcommit, this really is not a problem (although it may look like one at first).

Now, as the teams get started building the items on the backlog, they will also begin the process of slicing and reestimating these large items into increasingly smaller items. Called *backlog grooming,* this process will result in increasingly accurate estimates as the backlog items get smaller. But, here again we are protected by broad estimations of the largest epics on the backlog. Many of those items, when sliced into smaller items, will actually grow, while several others will actually get smaller.

In addition, when teams practice good story slice methods, the Product Owner will frequently find pieces of the original backlog item that simply do not need to be done in the current release. This ability to negotiate with the Scrum teams creates a significant ability to control the overall committed work, keeping it small enough to achieve the desired value in the anticipated timeframes.

To illustrate, imagine a large epic, originally sized at 89 story points, to build a new way for same-day surgery patients to provide all of their

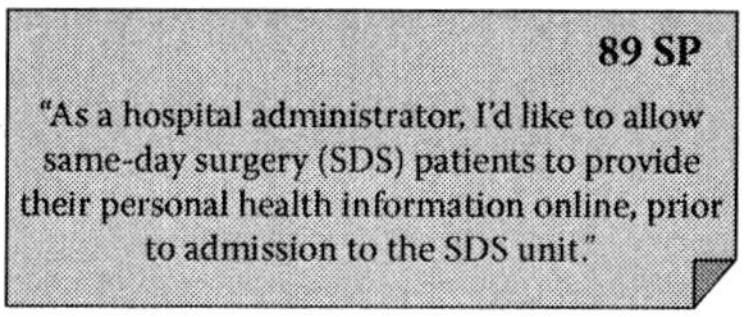

89 SP

"As a hospital administrator, I'd like to allow same-day surgery (SDS) patients to provide their personal health information online, prior to admission to the SDS unit."

FIGURE 14.4
An epic story sized at 89 story points.

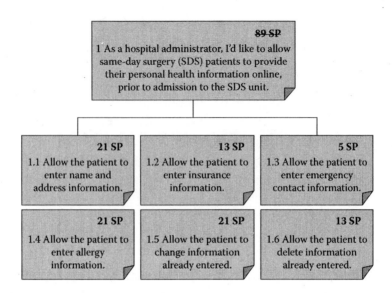

FIGURE 14.5

The epic story in Figure 14.4 sliced into smaller stories.

personal health information prior to being admitted to the hospital. So, our first user story looks like that in Figure 14.4.

Following the initial sizing of the team for Release Planning purposes, the Scrum team then does a round of story slicing, creating multiple smaller stories that reflect the overall functionality hinted at in the original story (Figure 14.4). The result of the slicing and estimation of the original story looks like Figure 14.5.

Note that the total size of the multiple smaller stories is 21 + 13 + 5 + 21 + 21 + 13 or 94 story points. This adjustment is common when a user story is sliced, I call the phenomenon "backlog swelling" because the backlog seems to grow slightly even though we aren't adding new content; however, as we keep slicing, we start to see stories in which the developers get more comfortable (and therefore reduce the effort) as well as stories that the Product Owner can easily decide to do without. Figure 14.6 shows what happens when we slice the stories again.

In Figure 14.6 you see some interesting effects. First, the Product Owner has apparently decided to delete the following stories:

- Story 1.1.3 (automated zip code lookup from street address): This sounded cool when the developers talked about it, but when the Product Owner saw the overall size becoming too large, she

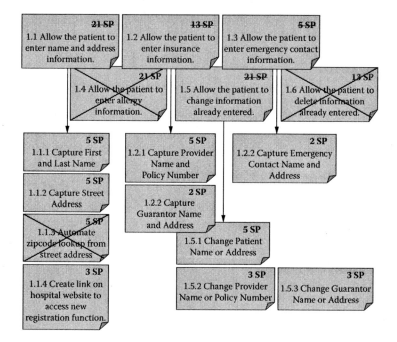

FIGURE 14.6
The epic story in Figure 14.1 sliced into smaller stories. Some stories are immediately deleted by the product owner.

deleted this story right away. "The patient can type his or her zip code," she said.

- Story 1.4 (allergy information): The Product Owner spoke with the head of nursing, and they decided that allowing patients to enter allergy information might be asking for some bad outcomes (incorrectly entered information). So, this story was deleted right away.
- Story 1.6 (delete information): The Product Owner decided that this could wait until the next release. For now, patients will be advised that information entered cannot be deleted, but will be reconfirmed on the day of the surgery, allowing a change at that time.

Some stories ended up being smaller than anticipated when the developers sliced them out. In particular, they noticed that they had to build name and address fields and validation logic for the patient, the guarantor (the person who is the policy holder of the insurance), and the emergency contact. They figured that the first effort (probably patient) would take the longest (5 story points), but the others would simply be cut-and-paste operations and were reduced to 2 story points each.

After the second slicing and review, the total size of the epic (now much more clearly defined than before) is 33 story points. These decisions have reduced the overall size of the epic by more than 50%.

Of course, it does not always work this way. In many cases, the total size of a sliced epic is equal to or more than its original estimate. But, when taken across 20 or 30 epics, many epics *do* slice down in ways that give the Product Owners and the Scrum teams ways to reduce the overall scope without losing any of the intended value. So, it is both a sound practice and an accurate one to estimate epics in terms of story points and then, as epics are sliced into smaller pieces, continue to create an increasingly accurate forecast of project completion.

HOW CAN I INCORPORATE USER INTERFACE STYLE GUIDES?

User interface (UI) style guides, like many other guidelines that are used to build a quality, consistent product, are simply examples of overarching function requirements that need to be followed during the normal course of software development. To make certain that something like this is effectively used, we need to take the following steps:

1. Make sure that the team understands the guidelines. Review them with the team. Make sure they understand why the guidelines are important. Give the team an opportunity to ask questions. Listen and, if necessary and possible, make changes.

2. Make the guidelines part of the DONEness criteria that all teams are using (e.g., "Ensure that any new or changed UI components are validated against the UI style guide"). Make sure that the team is reminded of the new requirement during the first couple of Sprints. The ScrumMaster should make a point of reminding the team during the Sprint. The Product Owner should make a point of checking it during Sprint Review. Failure to comply should result in backlog items being returned to the backlog.

3. Ensure that the guideline is (at least) briefly discussed during the team's retrospective meeting. Does the guideline make sense? Is it clear? Should it be changed?

HOW DO I MANAGE RISK IN THE AGILE PROJECT?

In traditional projects, we identify, track, and mitigate risk to reduce the impact of potential risks on the quality of the product and the timelines of the project. A risk management plan is created, and the project manager or the risk manager then becomes responsible for working with others on the project to identify when a risk has "fired" and then activating the plan to reduce the overall impact.

In agile development, risk is still a possibility. There is always a risk that we might lose a team member to a transfer; a substantial reprioritization of the Product Backlog may result in a termination of one or more Sprints and a loss of time; a particular technology may not work sufficiently, thus causing us to go to "plan B"; or a supplier may not be able to provide all of the needed resources, leaving the project team shorthanded and underskilled.

In agile development, I believe there are two levels of risk that need to be dealt with. The first is at the project level and is similar to the project risks of more traditional projects. The second is at the team level and is similar to traditional project risks, but our methods of handling those risks are a little different from before.

Let us deal first with project risks. The types of risks we need to deal with at the project level in the agile project are

- Organizational
  - The project lacks an effective sponsor.
  - Staffing is cut during the project.
  - Budget is cut during the project.
  - Management makes decisions that hurt team morale.
  - An external supplier takes too long to provide a deliverable.
- Personnel
  - Teams are understaffed due to delays getting the proper staffing.
  - Training is required to bring team members to minimal sufficiency.
  - Team members leave the project before completion.
  - Team members take an extended leave of absence during the project.
  - Key personnel are not sufficiently available.

- Process
  - Too much waste in the project causes slower-than-expected progress.

In dealing with these risks, it is going to be up to the organization to decide how much risk management is needed. At the same time, however, we have to look at these risks and consider them from an agile perspective. Let us look at the first one—the project lacks an effective sponsor.

Let us assume first that we are referring to managing the project even with an ineffective sponsor, not that we have to do something about the sponsor's ineffectiveness (I grant that this is also a legitimate possibility, but not for this exercise). Following traditional methods, we must ask the question, what is the potential impact of the risk of the ineffective sponsor on the project? In an agile project, we have to look at the sponsor's responsibilities: Does the sponsor manage the vision and direction of the product, or does he or she manage the teams that are building the product? Is the sponsor actually responsible for both the product *and* the people? In the case of the product vision, the project sponsor could have an impact on the project in terms of the prioritization of the Product Backlog or the team's understanding of the content of the Product Backlog. In the case of the sponsor being responsible for the development personnel, the sponsor could hire the wrong people, do or say things that hurt employee morale, or be ineffective in clearing large organization impediments that no one in the organization has the authority to deal with. In any case, this could be a horrendous situation.

In traditional risk management, the next thing we would do is determine the probability of loss and the potential size of the loss if the risk ends up happening. For example, in the case of the ineffective project sponsor, perhaps (since we know this sponsor from previous efforts) we rate the probability of loss at 75%. We also determine the likely impact to the project as 10 weeks. This means that our risk exposure is 7.5 weeks.

Table 14.5 shows a sample list of known risks for a project. This table also includes the probability of a risk occurring, the impact of the risk if it occurs, and the calculated exposure to the project (the product of the probability multiplied by the size of the impact).

When we compare this possible loss to other risks, we can prioritize the list and then decide what to mitigate and what to monitor as a low-priority risk. If we continue with this same process through the rest of the identified risks, we get a risk assessment table (sorted by exposure).

TABLE 14.5

A Sample List of Known Project Risks

Risk	Probability of Risk (%)	Size of Risk (Impact)	Risk Exposure (in weeks)
The project lacks an effective sponsor.	75	10	7.5
Staffing is cut during the project.	40	15	6.0
Budget is cut during the project.	35	10	3.5
An external supplier takes too long to provide a deliverable.	40	8	3.2
Management makes decisions that hurt team morale.	25	6	1.5

Personally, I prefer a slightly more "agile" twist to this method, discarding the concept of "size of loss" for something that works better for my sensibilities: high risk, medium risk, and low risk We can then determine how we want to react based on a combination of risk probability and risk impact. Following this method, a single, simple matrix suggests our actions (Table 14.6).

Table 14.6 shows a more agile approach to risk management (as compared with Table 14.5). Risks fall into a combination of impact and probability. By using both, you can identify a cell (which indicates an action to take). Cells marked "RED" need a risk management plan that is started as soon as possible. Cells marked "YELLOW" require monitoring and a plan, but no immediate action is taken. Cells without an entry are neither mitigated nor planned unless the risk occurs.

Using this matrix, the RED squares denote instances for which a risk mitigation plan must not only be created but also must be started at the earliest possible reasonable opportunity. YELLOW squares indicate risks that will be watched and planned, but nothing need occur until the risk presents itself. Squares with no content will be reacted to as the risk occurs.

TABLE 14.6

Risk Management by Impact and Probability

	High Impact	Medium Impact	Low Impact
High probability	RED	RED	YELLOW
Medium probability	RED	YELLOW	
Low probability	YELLOW		

TABLE 14.7

A Sample Risk Plan (Understaffed Teams)

Risk: Teams Are Understaffed Due to Delays Getting the Proper Staffing

Probability:	High
Impact:	High
Identification:	All teams are expected to have the resources as budgeted for the project from the beginning of Sprint 1.
Plan:	Should the teams not have budgeted resources as of Sprint 1 Planning, the following steps are to be taken:

1. Using 80% of the team's planned velocity as determined at Sprint 1 Planning, the Product Owner will determine the items on the Release Backlog that are threatened if the shortage continues for 1 sprint, 2 sprints, and 3 sprints.

2. The information from step 1 will be provided to the executive sponsor along with a list of the teams that are operating at less than budgeted capacity and the extent of that shortage.

3. The executive sponsor will make the decision whether or not to
   a. continue the project
   b. leave the staffing at current levels and accept the reduction in scope
   c. leave the staffing at current levels and add enough Sprints to make up for the shortage in resources
   d. escalate the staffing shortage to get back to the expected content as quickly as possible

4. Assuming the project is not cancelled, the portion of the backlog endangered by the resource shortage can be reassessed at the end of each Sprint and the decisions and expectations revisited as needed.

Therefore, any high-impact risk with a high or medium probability of occurring will require a risk mitigation plan to be devised and carried out at the earliest possibility. Any medium-impact risk with a high probability of occurrence also requires a plan. No low-risk items require any planning, although those with a high probability of occurrence at least require monitoring.

Thankfully, Scrum provides so many opportunities for visibility that monitoring risks and taking action are actually made simpler than in traditional projects. Let us take a look at a few examples.

Table 14.7 shows an identified risk with documentation for handling if there are delays getting the proper staffing.

Table 14.8 shows an identified risk with documentation for handling if an external supplier delivers behind schedule.

TABLE 14.8

A Sample Risk Plan (External Supplier is Late)

Risk: An External Supplier Takes Too Long to Provide a Deliverable

Probability:	Medium
Impact:	High
Identification:	Functionality to be provided by the supplier has been identified in the Release Backlog with backlog items that indicate "who will provide what by when." For example, a backlog item might read as follows: "Upgraded graphics card interface routines will be provided by GraphTek by May 15, 2011." Backlog items such as these, called "supplier items," will be tracked as indicated in the risk management plan.
Plan:	During each Sprint, the Scrum team will evaluate items that will likely be built during the next Sprint (this is done during the normal process of backlog grooming). If a supplier item is due during the next Sprint, the ScrumMaster will follow up with the supplier manager to determine if the deliverable is on schedule. Depending on the follow-up, the following steps will occur: If the deliverable is on schedule, the Scrum team will plan their next Sprint as normal, using the deliverable as appropriate when delivered. If the deliverable *may* be delayed, the Scrum team will plan the next Sprint as normal, bringing in the supplier item as a low-priority goal during the Sprint. There may also be an escalation to the supplier manager if appropriate. If the deliverable *will* be delayed, the Product Owner will reprioritize the supplier item based on the new anticipated delivery date. There may also be an escalation to the supplier manager if appropriate. For items requiring a longer lead time, the Scrum teams can be directed to look two or three Sprints ahead for supplier Items, rather than simply one Sprint.

Following each Sprint, the risk management plan can be reviewed and updated based on the outcomes of the previous Sprint. If possible, if a risk review can be held after the Sprint Reviews but before the Sprint Retrospective meetings, it might even be possible to introduce into the Sprint Retrospective meetings risk mitigation steps that the teams can discuss, solve, and carry forward into the next Sprint.

Within the Sprint, however, we take a different perspective on project risk. In short, risk management in the Sprint is "built in." We take a closer look at how this happens in this section. Let us start by looking at the types of risks that typically occur within the Sprint.

- Schedule
  - Team overcommits at Sprint Planning.
  - Team undercommits at Sprint Planning.
  - Team experiences a large number of defects, forcing them to decommit scope.
  - A key resource gets tied up on a single task, causing a cascade of failures along the rest of the Sprint Backlog.
- Requirements
  - Requirements are not clearly understood, which results in rework.
  - Requirements change during the Sprint, forcing changes in solution and approach.
- Team and personnel
  - Team members need time to learn unfamiliar software tools or environment.
  - Team members need time to learn unfamiliar hardware environment.
  - Team members do not work well together.
  - Team members lack the necessary skills to get the job done.
- Solution obstacles
  - The proposed solution does not perform or cannot satisfy the Product Owner's acceptance criteria.
  - The proposed solution cannot be enabled due to the design of other pieces of the product.
  - The proposed solution cannot be enabled without making significant changes to another portion of the product.
- Development environment
  - Errors in the integrated development environment (IDE) cause unexpected delays for the developers.
  - Tools necessary for development are not available on time.
  - Tools used by development do not work as expected.
  - Tools used by development do not provide planned productivity.
- Product problem
  - Errors in nightly builds consistently take the developers away from development and into support.
  - Errors in hourly builds consistently take the developers away from development and into support.
  - Poor quality or ineffective tests create delays in product integration or require developers to spend extra time in diagnosis.

Believe it or not, many of these risks are already built in to agile development practices. Let us eliminate them one by one so we can focus on the risks that remain.

Team over- or undercommits at Sprint Planning. During the Sprint, the team discusses over- and undercommitment with the Product Owner and adjusts the Sprint Backlog accordingly. In future Sprints, using the concept of velocity and "yesterday's weather" (Extreme Programming, XP), the team can more realistically plan their commitment.

Team experiences a large number of defects, forcing them to decommit scope. During the Sprint, this is handled as if the team overcommitted. They discuss the situation with the Product Owner and adjust the Sprint Goals accordingly. Work that cannot be done is returned to the Product Backlog. If the defect load was significant, the team will also likely spend time in their Sprint Retrospective trying to determine how it happened and what to do about it. Also, the team will use their velocity and yesterday's weather to ensure that they account for defect volume in future Sprints.

A key resource is tied up on a single task, causing a cascade of failures along the rest of the Sprint Backlog. During the Sprint, team members are encouraged (often required) to work with other team members, reducing the likelihood of getting stuck on a single task without its being noticed. In addition, the Daily Scrum often catches backlog items that are stalled, giving the rest of the team visibility to the problem and an opportunity to help address whatever is causing the problem.

Requirements are not clearly understood, resulting in rework. During and before the Sprint, the team spends time with the Product Owner to clarify the requirements. The Product Owner maintains a high degree of visibility to what the team is building so that, should the team misinterpret the requirements, the Product Owner can quickly assess and correct the problem.

Requirements change during the Sprint, forcing changes in solution and approach. During the Sprint, a requirements change often is communicated by the Product Owner, resulting in a negotiation with the Scrum Team to determine the nature of their new commitment. If the changed requirements result in an overcommitment of the Sprint Goal, backlog items will be returned to the Product

Backlog and removed from the Sprint commitment. If the changed requirements result in an undercommitment of the Sprint Goal, new work can be taken from the Product Backlog and added to the Sprint Backlog. If the changed requirements create so much change that the Sprint Goal is no longer effective, the entire Sprint can be terminated and replanned.

Team members need time to learn unfamiliar software tools, environments, or hardware environments, *or* team members lack the necessary skills to get the job done. During Sprint Planning, skill issues can be identified and tasks can be added to the Sprint Backlog to account for the training effort. Also, because agile development builds software incrementally, it is no longer necessary to learn everything all at once; training can be spread out over the course of several Sprints.

The proposed solution does not perform or cannot satisfy the Product Owner's acceptance criteria. During the Sprint, the inability of the team to satisfy the Product Owner's acceptance criteria will result in a renegotiation of the criteria with the Product Owner. The discussion might end with a renegotiation of the acceptance criteria to allow the team to pass at a lowered expectation. On the other hand, the renegotiation could result in an analysis story to investigate other alternatives that *would* satisfy the original acceptance criteria.

The proposed solution cannot be enabled due to the design of other pieces of the product, *or* the proposed solution cannot be enabled without making significant changes to another portion of the product. During the Sprint, should this condition be detected, the Scrum team and the Product Owner would work together to determine an acceptable solution to the problem. Between them, they can reprioritize the Product Backlog, add new Product Backlog items to modify other pieces of the product, negotiate out certain acceptance criteria, and modify story estimations.

Errors in the IDE cause unexpected delays for the developers, *or* tools necessary for development are not available on time, *or* tools used by development do not work as expected. During the Sprint, the team will quickly discover (usually as a result of Daily Scrum meetings) that they are collectively having difficulty with the IDE or tool. At this point, they will either devise a different solution or escalate the problem to management for assistance.

Errors in nightly builds consistently take the developers away from development and into support, *or* errors in hourly builds

consistently take the developers away from development and into support. During the Sprint, the team's time spent on defects will potentially cause a lessening of the team's velocity, which will in turn result in a conversation between the team and the Product Owner to adjust the team's commitment. In addition, the team should then spend time during the Sprint Retrospective determining what they should be doing to deal with the defects. In the meantime, the team's velocity will be lowered (by suggesting a smaller commitment, it is hoped) until they are able to complete more during the Sprint (preferably by reducing the number of defects encountered during the Sprint).

Poor quality or ineffective tests create delays in product integration or require developers to spend extra time in diagnosis. During the Sprint, the extra work caused by the ineffective tests is going to cause delays in getting committed backlog items to completion. This in turn is likely to cause a conversation between the team and the Product Owner to adjust the team's commitment. In addition, the team should then spend time during the Sprint Retrospective determining what they should be doing to deal with the defects. In the meantime, the team's velocity will be lowered (by suggesting a smaller commitment, it is hoped) until they are able to complete more during the Sprint (preferably by reducing the number of test failures encountered during the Sprint).

Another factor in agile development that tends to mitigate the impact of risks on the project schedule has to do with the estimation techniques often used when estimating user stories; you may need to determine whether these practices are in place in your organization. Specifically, when estimating user stories, teams are generally taught to estimate the "size" of story while considering the following:

- Complexity: Is this story relatively simple, or are there a lot of parts?
- Magnitude: How "big" is the story?
- Risk: What are the risks? Have we done something like this before? Does the Product Owner clearly understand the requirements? Do the tools we need to use cause a lot of extra problems?

When teams consider the risk of the backlog item, a greater risk assessment by the team will result in a larger estimation and, therefore, more time to resolve whatever problems might come up during the building of the backlog item. In fact, if the team determines that the Product Owner does not really understand the requirements, they may either ask that more time be spent on the item by the Product Owner before the team commits to the item, or they might ask that analysis stories be added to the backlog to understand the backlog item better (thus reducing the inherent risk). Scrum teams manage their own risk—this is one of the many advantages of self-managing teams—and can be more risk adverse or more risk tolerant simply based on the ability of the organization to accept modifications to the Scrum team's Sprint Goal.

Referring to the list of risks that can occur within the Sprint, did you notice the one risk *not* handled by the Scrum team? Here it is:

- Team members do not work well together.

While teams are expected to be self-managing, part of what we need the ScrumMaster and the management of the organization to do is help the team to learn how to work together, to provide training to team members who need it, and, when necessary, to change the team membership to create a better outcome. In other words, while the team takes responsibility for some of their inability to work together, management will usually need to lend a helping hand. So, let us assume from now on that the effectiveness of individuals working together to be a team is actually a *project-level risk*. In doing so, let us approach this risk from the more traditional standpoint:

Risk: Team members do not work well together.
Probability: High
Impact: High

For demonstrative purposes, let us assume there are many new teams on the project. Therefore, the possibility that the teams may not work well together is fairly high. On a project for which only a few teams are new, you could successfully argue "medium" probability. Likewise, if you have many proven and effective teams, you could easily argue "low" probability. On the matrix in Table 14.6, that means that we would have to put a mitigation plan in place for both the high- and medium-probability cases. We would still have to monitor the situation on the low-probability case—but doesn't that make sense? Your entire project is reliant on the effectiveness of your teams; if they are not performing, you are going to have problems. In this light, monitoring the teams is only prudent.

So, while many types of risks are built in many agile practices and the Scrum framework, many others still require monitoring. To deal with the one discussed (team members do not work well together), we would probably want to put some kind of monitoring in place to determine if the team is functioning well. We will also need some idea of what steps we will take should we find a teamwork problem. We might even want to do something, like workshops or team-building exercises, before the project begins to lessen the probability of a teamwork issue.

Risk management in an agile project is not terribly different from risk management in a more traditional project. The key is to understand which risks are project risks and should be addressed at the project level and which risks are in-Sprint risks and are already handled by agile and Scrum practices. If you are not sure which is which, handle the risks at the project level and then see if the Scrum teams are already addressing them in their normal activities. If so, you have the choice of either continuing to monitor the in-Sprint risks or just letting the teams do it.

WHAT ABOUT THE PROJECT MANAGER?

Scrum only provides for three roles: ScrumMaster, Product Owner, and the Scrum team. To the extent that we expect our Scrum teams to build high-quality product by following the direction of the Product Owner, those three roles are usually sufficient. However, the logistics of the situation become increasingly complicated as the number of teams grows while the organization itself continues to operate as before (this will be discussed in more detail).

There are multiple Product Owners to work with, and in many large organizations, more teams and departments have to be collaborated with during the typical project. Collaborating Scrums[2] can handle some of the logistical needs, but as they become increasingly complex, I see a need for someone who "brings it all together." You can call this person a release manager, a project manager, a line manager. It does not really matter what you call them. What is important is what they do for the large agile project. What is also important to note here is that everything I list as a responsibility of the "project manager" could be done by anyone on the project. The responsibilities can even be shared or rotated across multiple people on the project.

However, when the "agile project manager" is used, I believe that the fundamental role is to provide support to the Scrum teams by fulfilling at least some of the following functions:

- Consolidation of project status reporting to organization management
- Coordination with external stakeholder teams (e.g., beta management, quality management)
- Coaching ScrumMasters (if possible)
- Helping keep Product Owner teams on track
- Helping with realignment of resources when team structure needs to be changed

I have one further note on this. I mentioned that the logistics of the situation become increasingly complicated as the organization transitions to agile development but keeps the rest of the business process as before. What I mean by this is that an organization can be agile or not agile with relative ease (how successful the organization will be in delivering quality software is a different question). But, when an organization is *partially* agile, you will see the need for a "conduit" between the new practices and the old—the project manager.

As more of the organization moves to agile practices, you should see decreasing need for someone to manage the projects as the organization incorporates more of its daily operation into self-managing teams.

HOW DO I START A PRODUCT FROM SCRATCH?

If you are in the position of building a whole new product or application in an agile environment, I envy you. I know that sounds a little strange, but think about it: You have an opportunity to start fresh: no test automation problems, no upset customers, no huge defect queues. You do not have to worry about features that got into your product that no one really wants but no one will let you take out. Chances are the only expectations you have to worry about resetting right now are your own.

Step 1: Create the Product Vision

Assuming you have the rough idea for a new product, we can start by nailing down the rough vision, values, and goals that you have for the product. This is an important, yet often overlooked, step in the product development process. It starts by answering these questions:

1. **Who is the product for?** Who are the users? What can you tell me about them? Age? Education? Likes and dislikes? The more you know about your users, the better a job you can do building the product and prioritizing features.
2. **What is the product budget?** What are we willing to spend on the product?
3. **What need are we filling?** As Henry Ford put it, "The market is never saturated with a good product, but it is very quickly saturated with a bad one." Understand what it is your customers actually want. Then, and only then, can you actually provide it again and again.
4. **What is our product name?** While you do not actually need to know yet, I have seen a lot of products go to market with working names and project keywords in the code and on the printed reports for the product. These often pop up at inopportune times and cost time and money to fix later. If you know it now, you can avoid problems of rewriting or redesigning later.
5. **What type of product is it?** There are many possible answers for this question, and all aspects should be explored. How will it be licensed? What type of platform or platforms will it run on? What does it need to do and look like in its first version? What does it need to do 4 or 5 years from now? Are we replacing an existing product?
6. **When do we need the product on the market?** Is there some kind of market event or events that we need to worry about? Is a competitor trying to get something to market as well? Doe we want to have demo versions ready for important conferences?

Now, collecting, reviewing, discussing, and finally deciding on the right answers to these questions should take you anywhere from several days to several weeks. Do not discount this piece of the work; it is extremely important that you get this part right. Once you are comfortable with the answers, you can move on to the next part: the capabilities.

Step 2: Build the Initial Product Backlog

When we talk capabilities, we are talking about the really big, obvious features that your product needs to possess. Most products, even the really big ones, only have three or four major capabilities. Everything else either supplements the capability, allows different capabilities to interact, or supports the product so that the capabilities work properly. Let us look at a few examples of capabilities, supplementers, integrators, and supporters. We use, as an example, a Web-based auction site.

Capabilities
- Allow items to be placed on the site for bidding.
- Allow people to place bids on items.
- Coordinate the movement of money to the owner and product to the bidder.

Supplementers (items that add to the capability, but are not part of the core critical functionality; some supplementers are added to ensure that the product satisfies applicable regulations)
- Allow pictures of the item to display in a slideshow manner.
- Allow buyer to keep track of purchases during the lifetime of the buyer's account.
- Allow buyer to comment on the seller's performance during the sale.

Integrators (items that tie capabilities together when they need to interact)
- Allow seller to see the current state of the bidding.
- Allow seller to cancel auction.
- Allow buyer to "buy now" and end the auction.

Supporters (functions that support the capabilities but are not part of the capabilities)
- Allow users to sign on.
- Allow users to sign off.
- Allow buyers to generate a report of their purchases.

When you build a new product, you will generally start with the capabilities and go from there. Certainly, you might know you want support for a "user account" feature along with internal security to keep the wrong people from using the wrong functions. But, it is from here that the initial Product Backlog will come together, be prioritized, and then sliced into

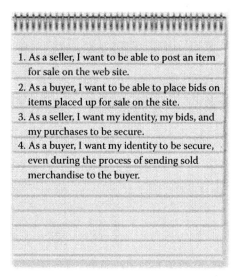

1. As a seller, I want to be able to post an item for sale on the web site.
2. As a buyer, I want to be able to place bids on items placed up for sale on the site.
3. As a seller, I want my identity, my bids, and my purchases to be secure.
4. As a buyer, I want my identity to be secure, even during the process of sending sold merchandise to the buyer.

FIGURE 14.7
New Product Backlog built from a list of capabilities.

increasingly smaller pieces of functionality. So, for our Web-based auction site, our initial Product Backlog might start like Figure 14.7.

Before we get our Scrum teams involved, we will do a little more grooming to give our teams something for a "functional" grasp. Here is what the list might look like after a little work:

- As a seller, I want to post a simple item without pictures for sale.
- As a seller, I want to post an item with a single picture.
- As a seller, I want to post an item with multiple pictures.
- As a buyer, I want to review items placed up for bids.
- As a buyer, I want to be able to place a bid on an item up for sale.
- As a seller, I want to sign on to use the system.
- As a seller, I want a strong password required to validate my log in.
- As a winning buyer, I want to be able to protect my name from the buyer, such that they get only a "ship to" address for the item.

This list may not be complete, but it truly does not have to be. The important thing to ask yourself is this - are the most important items that I need on this list? No? Then simply add them. For example, on reviewing this list, we quickly discover that there's no way to pay for anything. So, let

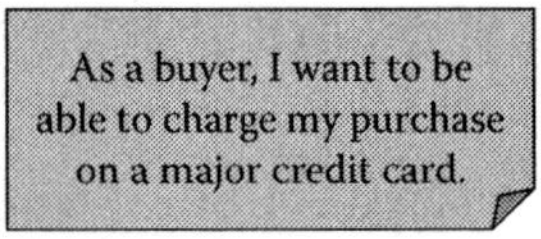

> As a buyer, I want to be
> able to charge my purchase
> on a major credit card.

FIGURE 14.8
A user story adding to the Product Backlog the ability to pay for items.

us add a backlog item to allow us to charge the purchase on a major credit card (Figure 14.8).

That is all you have to do to get started. Nothing more to add right now (remember, you can always add more later). Let us continue to the next step.

Step 3: Create the Initial Architectural Design

It is time to get your Scrum team involved; from this point, you want to keep them involved in any changes that you make to the Product Backlog. At this point in the project, before the team starts building anything, you want them to do two things to the backlog. First, it is their responsibility to assign effort estimates to every item; without that, it is difficult to plan a release in terms of how much can be done by the deadline or what date should be set for the first usable version of the new product. Second, you will want the team to create an architectural design for the product based on what they can determine from the backlog and by discussing the product with you.

My recommendation at this stage of product development is that you have one or two Scrum teams assigned to the product development, and that you use both teams to do the effort estimation and to create the initial architectural design. Your architects can lead the discussions; your testers, developers, and analysts can provide insight and perspective, as well as help create the design documentation for the product.

Now, I know this is different from what you may have done in the past, but think of all the products you have worked on for which you have heard complaining about how the architects do not work well with the developers, how the architecture does not provide what the product needs, and how the developers never use the architecture properly. Anybody with any schooling in agile development will tell you almost immediately that the problem with this situation is that the lines of communication between the architects and developers just are not there. The easiest way to fix this problem is to have them all work together—blasphemous, I know. But there it is. Architects may have specialized knowledge, but that is no reason to separate them from the rest of the team. Everyone has their specializations, but they work best when they work together.

Let us return to the architecture design for a moment. Once the initial draft of the design is complete and the team (or teams) feel comfortable moving forward, let them. The truth is that the architecture design is *never* finished. You and the teams should consider the design a working document. The reason for this is simple: The purpose for the architecture to exist is to facilitate the application functionality. In other words, we create architecture functionality *only* to support application functionality. And, since we expect the application functionality to change over time, we also expect the architecture functionality to change over time (although, truthfully, a good lightweight architecture will change less over time unless the application undergoes a radical change). Therefore, the architecture design is used to set a guideline and a rough plan—a plan that we expect will change from Sprint to Sprint as we build more of the application.

Step 4: Groom the Product Backlog

At this point, it is time to take what you know about your product and what your teams have determined from their research and prioritize the Product Backlog to start getting the highest-value (or, potentially, the highest-risk) items in progress as soon as possible. You should also expect an outcome of the architecture design effort to be a number of backlog items of a more technical nature. Your team can help you identify the order in which the items need to be done.

Your team will do more of the work at this point, taking the highest-priority items, breaking them down into increasingly smaller pieces with help from your knowledge of how you want the items to function and then building the small items during Sprints.

Step 5: Moving Forward

Your job at this point is multifaceted. You should plan to

1. Continue to add new items to the backlog as you learn more about what you want the product to do. Remember, as you build capabilities, those capabilities will likely need supporting items, integrating items, and supplemental items that shine up your capabilities for the general market.

2. Continue to prioritize the backlog, getting help from your Scrum teams as needed to deal with the more technical items on the list.

3. Continue to work directly with your Scrum teams. They are going to build what you ask them to, but sometimes there are differences in interpretation, and sometimes you learn more about what you want the product to look like and how you want it to function when you see it partially built.

4. Get customers involved with the development effort. Start by showing them what has been built so far and getting their feedback. Talk to them about what will be coming next and in the first release and see what they have to say about it. If you find customers that have a really good vision and might work well with your Scrum teams, consider getting them directly involved with your teams.

5. Participate in Sprint Reviews and encourage discussion regarding what was built and what you want to see next. Reprioritize your list based on the outcomes of the discussion and then repeat step 4.

Most important, be a smart Product Owner. If you find yourself in the enviable position of being a Product Owner for a new product, do not make the mistakes (or allow them to happen) that other Product Owners and product managers have been making and allowing for years. Make a priority of value and quality.

1. Make sure you work with your Scrum teams during backlog grooming to slice backlog items down to small pieces and then look carefully at those pieces. Think about them. Which of them do you really need in the next release of the product? Which of them would actually allow the product to be both competitive and desirable? Which ones are simply cool? Decide carefully and either deprioritize or delete the items you do not need.

2. Insist that your developers keep the product fully testable and that the product can be automatically and completely tested every night. Some Product Owners do not put any value on the testability of their product, and then wonder why their developers cannot get the product out the door at the end of the project. Trust me, I have seen a tremendous amount of productivity lost every Sprint as a result of builds that took too long and tests that did not work properly. And I have seen incredible improvements in productivity when those tests were improved.

3. Insist on DONEness at all times. Do not allow your teams to look at DONEness as an optional item. The difference between getting a backlog item to DONE and just getting a backlog item to work is the same difference we see when children do their homework but forget to check their work; the paper is complete, but the answers are all wrong. In some cases, it could be the same as the difference between having your auto mechanic fix your car correctly or fix your car so that it runs for a short period of time. The car works in the beginning (during the "demo") but then fails when you can least afford it. Consider also the long-lasting effects of poor work. Defects, found later, become much more expensive to fix. Fixing your grade after a few blundered homework assignments requires much more work than simply checking your homework. Software development is no different. We can strive to get it right the first time, or we can spend much more time and money getting it right later. If a backlog item is not DONE at Sprint Review, it must go back in the Product Backlog to be completely finished in a future Sprint.

4. There may be times when you will decide to "compromise" DONEness. For example, there is an important demo for a customer or a conference in your industry coming up, *but* the key feature we want to demonstrate will take too long and cannot be done in time for the customer or the conference. Your Scrum team tells you that if they just stick to the bare minimum work, cutting all of the specification and testing, they could produce a working version of the feature that will work along a predefined script. In these situations, the potential value you gain in sales may, in fact, be worth allowing your Scrum teams to cut some corners. When they do this, the work that they do not do (the specifications and the testing) become "technical debt." Technical debt is defined as work that should be done to satisfy DONEness and other system qualities (testability, scalability, portability, etc.) as well as the defects that result from the work that is not done. In the financial world, it is considered good practice to carry a little debt in favor of better opportunities (the potential increased sales from the customer or the conference), but to service that debt regularly to keep it small and manageable. In the software world, we manage the technical debt that we knowingly incur by creating a new backlog item and putting on it the work that we deliberately did not do and then getting that work done at the earliest possible opportunity. In the example, we incur some technical debt by not writing

the specifications and doing the proper testing for the important feature. We will then create a backlog item that indicates which specifications were not updated and which code and functionality were not properly covered with tests, and then we prioritize that new item *as high on the backlog as possible.* In the best case, the specifications are updated and the testing is completed in the next Sprint, while the salespeople (carefully) demonstrate the earlier version of the feature to the customer or at the conference.

REFERENCE

Schiel, James A. 2010. *Enterprise-Scale Agile Software Development.* Boca Raton, FL: CRC Press.

ENDNOTES

1. Do not bother looking for this on the Internet; I just created the term for this discussion.
2. These are daily Scrum-like meetings that consist of individuals from multiple teams and are used to coordinate related activities across multiple teams.

15

Agile Development Dysfunctions

INTRODUCTION

Agile development is hard to do. It may appear easy to understand in many instances, but the truth is that agile development challenges much of what we used to do as developers and managers. As a result, many organizations attempting to adopt agile practices tend to see the surface of the practices but fail to see or comprehend how and why those practices work the way they do. So, we experience dysfunctional uses of agile development. In this chapter, we review many types of dysfunctions, what causes them, and if possible, what to do about them.

Remember that dysfunctions come in many variations but frequently have the same underlying cause. Look deeply: Even if the description of the circumstances does not match yours, does it feel similar? Also, understand that most dysfunctions are not deliberate; they are not caused by people who do not agree with agile development or are deliberately sabotaging your efforts to be more agile. Most dysfunctions are caused by people who simply have not been able to grasp the whole picture. Once they see what they are doing incorrectly, they will often quickly fix the mistake and become that much better for the effort.

WE DO FUNCTIONAL SPECIFICATIONS AND USE AGILE FOR DESIGN/BUILD: IS THAT WRONG?

To the question of whether it is wrong to provide functional specifications and use agile for the design and build, the short answer is a resounding "absolutely yes." It is so far from agile development that you are not likely

181

to experience any of the benefits of agile development. The long answer is more complicated.

Agile development is all about the frequent delivery of valuable software to customers. If you are writing all of your functional specifications first, how long will it be before you start delivering valuable software to your customer? But, that is only the obvious problem. Let us look deeper.

Why do we want to deliver software frequently and early? Think about it this way: When was the last time you had a customer who knew exactly what he or she wanted from you *before* you started building it? More than this, once you started building the software, when was the last time your customer had no changes for you? Here is one more question for you: When was the last time your specifications perfectly matched what you produced, and you did not have to change the specifications once?

Now, sure, there are probably a couple of people out there who will say, "Yes, my customers know what they want; they never change their minds, and my functional specifications are perfect when I build the software." For those few people saying "yes," I would suggest that you either have an unusual relationship with your customers or perhaps you have clearly known software requirements and a clearly understood technical environment. If either or both are true, keep reading, because agile development will work even better for you than for others.

For the rest of us, I am not suggesting that our customers are incompetent or that as analysts or developers we all could use significant improvement. What I am saying is this: Software development is the only engineering practice in existence for which we develop something (software products) from nothing more than ideas. In all other engineering practices, you have plans, you have inventory, and you have a finished product. If you are building a bridge, you know pretty much what you are going to build before you start. It is the same with building a car, a house, a swing set. We can draw pictures; we know what it is going to look like before we start—not so with software. You can draw all the pictures you want, but it is when you build it that your customer sees the real value. It is when you build it that things you did not even think of happen. It is when you build it that things do not work that you never thought were going to cause a problem.

By writing the functional specifications first, what you are really doing is ensuring a substantial amount of rework during the actual writing and testing of the software. Why? As you build software, your customers will see things they did not see before. They will see things and tell you that you did not build them they way they wanted you to build them. They will change their minds about earlier decisions—all because nothing is more effective for your customers than seeing working software. Now, you get to change your software *and* your functional specifications.

Similarly, as you build your software, you will discover things you did not expect while writing the functional specifications. You may need to make a function work differently from the way you planned. You may need to drop a function entirely. When these changes occur, you will find yourself changing both your software *and* your functional specifications.

Given all this, and the fact that we have all dealt with technical surprises and changing customer desires, would it not make more sense to build the functional specifications at the same time we are building the software? When we write the functional specifications well in advance of the actual software, what we are actually doing is making many functional and technical decisions long before we need to. This violates a significant premise of lean development: to "defer decisions until the last reasonable moment."

In agile development, what we do instead is discuss the features we are about to build (usually about one iteration in advance of actually building the feature). We take notes, draw pictures, discuss (and sometimes argue) approaches. Then, when we actually build the software, we frequently check with the customer, showing what we have built, incorporating as much of the customer's feedback as makes sense into the software. Of course, while we are building software, we are also writing the functional specifications. By building software and specifications at the same time and working frequently with our customers, we eliminate a lot of rework both in the software and in the functional specifications.

By the very nature of what we build, we cannot know everything there is to know "up front," that is, before we build. In fact, experience has shown us that for the typical development effort, we actually know little beyond the most obvious details when we start writing our functional specifications. By writing the functional specifications earlier than the code (or tests, or anything else for that matter), we actually set ourselves up for considerably more rework, which in the end means that your functional specifications will cost more but will not provide any additional value.

I CONSTANTLY HAVE TO REMIND MY TEAM ABOUT DONENESS

The problem of constantly reminding your team about DONEness actually comes in many flavors. Your version might instead go like this: "I constantly have to remind my team about

- finishing the required documentation and getting it reviewed."
- writing enough unit and functional tests that the code is properly covered and thoroughly tested."
- making a serious effort to complete the backlog items they committed to do."

If you are hearing complaints like this, it is possible that the problem you are experiencing is related to team self-management, something that is absolutely crucial to a well-functioning Scrum team.

A team, as defined by the definitive volume *Agile Software Development with Scrum* (Schwaber, p. 38) is "responsible for meeting the goal to which it commits" and "assumes the authority necessary to meet their commitments." When a team is properly self-managing, you should see them making progress in three main areas:

1. Self-organization around the team commitment. What I mean by this is that, for every backlog item that the team commits to during Sprint Planning, they determine who is going to do the work and how the work is to be done. During the Sprint, teams will ensure that all required processes are followed, will monitor the progress of the backlog items they have committed to, and will work directly with the Product Owner when their commitment is in danger of not being realized.
2. Controlling the team membership. Some teams actually form themselves around product features; others bring in new members by consensus. In many organizations, team members participate in the interviewing and hiring decision process, giving them at least some control over what kind of individual is added to the team.
3. Influencing other teams and the organization. Good Scrum teams realize that they are dependent on the success of other Scrum teams in the organization. On a project of six Scrum teams, the resulting

product is really only as good as the performance of the weakest Scrum team. Some teams work hard to ensure that new practices and practice improvements are communicated to other teams to ensure that everyone can benefit.

But, this will not happen all at once.

It is not at all uncommon for a team to take some time before they realize that they are actually responsible for the work that they are doing. You will frequently find instances when the team should be responsible for something, but they usually forget to follow through. Some typical examples include

- Forgetting aspects of DONEness for some or all backlog items— which includes forgetting to write unit tests or functional tests, forgetting documentation-related tasks, and not meeting all of the acceptance criteria for a backlog item, even though the item is positioned as DONE at the end of the Sprint
- Frequently forgetting to update the Sprint Backlog tasks on a daily basis
- Allowing or requiring people outside the team (particularly management) to make administrative or technical decisions for the team

Getting a team to self-management can be simple or nearly impossible, depending on the team and the organization in which they work. For the rare team and organization, it is just a matter of explaining what it means to be self-managing; while there may be a false start or two, these teams grow into the concept of self-management rather quickly. For the majority of new Scrum teams, it will take time and patience. Several things need to be happen for a team to become self-managing; some of the things you will need to do to bring most teams to a more self-managing state are discussed next.

Train

Do not expect teams to be self-managing just because you told them that they need to be self-managing. For most of us, just saying "Go self-manage!" is not going to cause any new shift in thinking. Training a team to self-manage means, among other things, that they need to be aware of their responsibilities as a team. While there is more to it than this, it really

186 • *The ScrumMaster Study Guide*

does come down to this: The Product Owner sets the vision, the direction, and the priority—the Scrum team builds the product. That sounds straightforward enough, but let us take a look at what it means to "build the product." Here is a short list:

- The value required by the Product Owner is fully realized (i.e., all of the acceptance criteria have been satisfied).
- Nothing else that already worked has been broken by the addition of this new feature.
- All related code has been written, tested, reviewed, and checked in to the proper directory location.
- All related specifications have been created or updated, reviewed (and approved where appropriate), and checked in to the proper directory location.
- All related customer documentation has been created or updated, reviewed (and approved if appropriate), and checked in to the proper directory location.
- If necessary, backlog items have been created to echo similar functional additions or modifications in other supported releases.
- All associated unit tests have been written or updated, reviewed, and checked in to the proper directory locations.
- When executed, all unit tests run successfully, and the code coverage of the related production code stays at or above 90%, or whatever value the organization is using (which could vary from module to module, product to product, release to release).
- All associated functional tests have been written or updated, reviewed, and checked in to the proper directory locations.
- When executed, all functional tests run successfully.

This list does not include the administrative responsibilities of the team, such as keeping the task list up to date, recording their actual hours (not required by Scrum, but something that most teams do for accounting purposes), evaluating their commitment and negotiating with the Product Owner, providing status reports on a regular basis to management, and following through on retrospective decisions from previous Sprints.

Teams cannot be expected to self-manage if they are not aware of what it is they are supposed to be responsible for managing. Provide this information to the team when they are formed and plan on following up and repeating much of this information several times during the first few Sprints.

Trust

Teams who do not trust the organization do not self-manage. Taking responsibility is difficult when you do not know how the organization is going to respond to mistakes or when you cannot trust the organization to be consistent. Making it harder are the various dysfunctional relationships that often exist in the typical development organization: Management distrusts programmers, programmers distrust management, programmers distrust testers, testers distrust programmers, customers distrust everybody involved in software development, and so on. There are many reasons for distrust, and all of those have to be at least partially overcome for teams to truly begin self-management.

Trust can often be gained through empathy, by bringing team members together and allowing them to work together, to see what each other has to do, and to help each other deal with their problems. This is not always limited to the developers; I have seen several instances of managers moving out of their offices and into team rooms to be more available.

Try sitting the team down on a regular basis to discuss how things are going within the team and across the organization; just getting them talking will go a long way toward getting the team to work more effectively. You might even want to go so far as providing food for the team during meetings to lighten the stress a bit.

In addition, avoid trying to place blame for something that goes wrong on a specific person on the team. In an environment in which you are trying to emphasize shared responsibility, trust, and teamwork, the last thing you will want to allow is a witch hunt. The motto in a trusting environment must be, "the team fails and succeeds together."

Motivate

No one will be terribly tempted to do anything if he or she is not motivated to do the work in the first place. All of us long to realize the wisdom of Confucius: "Choose a job you love, and you will never have to work a day in your life." For those of us doing what we love, motivation is generally not a problem. For others, however, the lack of motivation is demonstrated in a variety of procrastination techniques, like putting off or entirely skipping uninteresting tasks or responsibilities. In any case, unmotivated personnel are extremely unlikely to become self-managing.

Motivating an unmotivated team, as with building trust, takes time and patience. It starts by getting someone on the team to set an example and be a role model. This person always contributes at meetings, always works with others on the team, and always focuses on getting backlog items done as quickly as possible with the highest possible quality.

The Product Owner can provide a lot of help as well. It is absolutely essential for the Product Owner to sit down with the team and share with them a vision for the product and how important the work is that the team is doing. What can also be effective is for the Product Owner to get the team involved in problems that he or she needs help with and to get the team's active involvement in solving those problems.

During team retrospectives, make sure that some time is spent recognizing the good things that individuals on the team accomplished. I have facilitated many retrospectives over the past several years, and I almost always have to force the team to recognize not only the good things that happened during the Sprint but also the good people who did them. Most teams are more than happy to criticize their efforts and talk about things that went wrong; getting them to recognize those people who did well takes an extra effort. Spend just a few minutes and ask each person on the team to thank someone for something that he or she did during the Sprint. It may initially be a little uncomfortable, but that extra effort will pay for itself in short order.

Managers and other interested stakeholders should reserve time during their busy schedules to attend daily standup meetings, Sprint Planning meetings, and Sprint Review meetings. Listen to the team members talk; invite them to explain their problems. Coach the team to solutions, rather than solving problems for the team. When necessary, change organizational policies and procedures to improve the team's ability to get things done.

Discipline

Agile development requires a significant degree of discipline to work properly. Heavyweight processes do not create quality software; lightweight processes do not create quality software. No matter how hard you try, no matter what you plan, quality software comes from skilled, disciplined developers. Your Scrum teams need to incorporate a significant degree of self-discipline to truly be effective. But, of course, saying the word *discipline* to a Scrum team is similar to saying "don't think, follow the rules."

The challenge in coaching an undisciplined Scrum team is to do so in a manner that teaches them that discipline does not limit them; it actually will help them to be even more successful. In the words of Stephen Covey (Covey, p. 74), "the undisciplined are slaves to moods, appetites, and passions." Teams that allow themselves to be governed by whatever mood they happen to be in on a particular day are destined to experience variable quality and unexpected surprises forever.

On the other hand, teams that have learned self-discipline control their own destiny. Teams that govern their actions by doing what needs doing find themselves recording success after success. They find better ways to work and fully leverage those improvements. They attack problems given to them by their Product Owners, and they do not slow down until the problems are completely solved.

Getting teams to be self-disciplined is, again, a process requiring patience and perseverance. We start by recognizing that, as a team, there are times when we wish we could work on more interesting things. We recognize that writing tests is not fun, and running them repeatedly is not glamorous. Having recognized and admitted to all of this, however, we then turn the team's attention to writing quality software—but not just as an affirmation. We need to discuss it as it really appears: as defects. Does the team like working on defects? Do they enjoy having managers and customers knocking on their doors demanding that they work late to fix defects? Do they enjoy working on something interesting, only to be interrupted by a defect that demands their attention? Do they look forward to working on month after month of defect repair at the end of the project?

In addition, the team needs to look at their own professional pride. Is it their intention as a career goal to write substandard software? Is that why they took all those classes and read all those books on good programming design and technique? Do they have pride in their work, or is it just something to fill the hours between 8 and 5? As you might imagine, these are important questions to ask, and in fact, when you get serious answers like, "Yes, I'm just doing this to get paid," you might consider inviting that individual to find another job. Besides the fact that it does not make sense to have someone working on your project who does not want to be there, the person's very presence can become a toxic influence on the rest of the team.

Now, how can we measure how successful we are at being self-disciplined? The easiest way to answer this question is to ask a different one: What is the most obvious sign of our lack of discipline? When answering this question, be sure to keep the "sign" direct and immediate. What I mean by this (and I hold this to be true for most metrics) is that you want to measure things that are direct and immediate results of the behavior you are trying to measure. For example, perhaps a team feels like all of the defects they are having to deal with are a result of their lack of discipline. This may be true, but the reporting of defects is often done by other people after the team completes the feature. Worse, there are many possible causes of a defect, from interaction with other components in the software product to mistakes in the acceptance criteria (detailed requirements). So, we cannot really say that every defect is directly caused by a lapse in self-discipline. Similarly, because the defect can be reported days, if not weeks, after the team is done with the feature, defects do not demonstrate clear and immediate evidence of a problem with self-discipline. We need to look for something more obvious. For example, self-discipline usually results in some of the following:

- Tasks have not been updated (in terms of hours remaining or overall status).
- Backlog items are marked as DONE when there are elements of DONEness not yet completed.
- Too many backlog items are in progress at the same time; generally, a Scrum team should not be working on more than two or three backlog items at the same time.
- Team members are missing from or late to team meetings

For each of these scenarios, we can easily measure the impact. For example, tasks not updated can often be discovered during the Daily Scrum meeting or via a little investigation by the ScrumMaster after or before the Daily Scrum. Tasks found not to be up to date can be ticked (with a little checkmark on the task or a comment in a tool). At the end of the Sprint, the marks can be counted and used to see how much the team has improved.

Similarly, a quick count, each day, of the number of backlog items in an "in progress" status can yield a metric that will show how good the team is getting at finishing backlog items before they start new ones.

Once you get a team interested in measuring their self-discipline and taking steps to improve it, more than half of the work is done (as is often said, "realization of a problem is half the battle"). Ongoing monitoring and coaching will help ensure that the team continues to make progress.

WHAT DO I DO IF THE FUNCTIONAL MANAGER IS STILL ASSIGNING TASKS WITHIN THE SPRINT?

In the Scrum framework, we want to encourage our teams to be as self-managing as possible. We do this for several reasons, not the least of which is that we want our teams to be committed to the entire process of building a product—from discussing the functional requirements, to defining a solution, to building that solution. When teams are held responsible for managing themselves to these commitments, they usually perform well. However, when a manager steps in and decides who is going to work on what, he or she is taking away responsibility from the team for getting the work done properly. The manager takes away the team's commitment and replaces it with compliance in the form of just "doing the tasks I have been assigned."

In addition, we also lose the team's ability to react to changes or unexpected deviations in the anticipated requirements. Since the manager has decided who will work on what, the team no longer feels comfortable adapting as the circumstances require and will always go back to the manager for reassignment. This is a very inefficient mode of working, as the team's ability to react and adapt is now limited by the manager.

If you have a manager assigning tasks within a Scrum team, the first thing to do (as always) is train. The same thing is true of managers as is true of employees: If something is not getting done correctly, it is either because the employee does not have the skills, or the employee does not have the right attitude. We deal with skills through training; we deal with attitude through performance management. So, we assume that the problem that this manager is suffering from is a lack of proper training, and we sit down with the manager and explain not only how a Scrum framework is supposed to work, but also what happens when the manager manages the Scrum team (as described in this section).

Of course, with a manager, it is also wise to ask why he or she is managing the Scrum team in this manner. There may be a reason that, despite the training, the manager feels assigning tasks is a necessity. In that case, you should review with the manager both the proper form of managing Scrum teams (Schiel 2010) and how he or she might alleviate his or her concerns about the team in a manner that is less destructive to an agile mode of development.

For example, you may run across a manager who tells you that he or she knows quite well how to manage a Scrum team, but the particular team the manager is dealing with is new to agile and junior at the same time; left to their own devices, the team would not get anything done. The response to this situation is to look at what the manager is trying to accomplish. The manager is right in stating that a new team (and a junior team to boot) requires more attention, but it is the type of attention the manager is providing that is causing the problem. In this particular case (and, frankly, with most cases of this sort), the manager has confused guidance and coaching with management and control. The answer for this team is for the manager not to tell the team what to do, but rather to help the team learn how to do it on their own, without supervision. More specifically, instead of assigning tasks to individuals on the team, the manager should be helping the team to learn how to volunteer for tasks, to spontaneously create small subteams to work together on a backlog item. The manager should be coaching the team to understand that it is not about getting the tasks done; it is about getting the backlog items done. How the team does it is not nearly as important as that the team does it and gets it done.

Of course, in the end, you may simply find yourself faced with a manager who understands it but refuses to do it. In this instance, you want to be sure that the agile transition planning of the organization includes a process for handling personnel who demonstrate a complete lack of desire to even try doing agile development. The process may include the opportunity to transfer the individual out of the organization and may even go so far as punitive steps (up to and including termination) should the employee fail to comply with the wishes of the organization to introduce agile development.

WHAT IF A MANAGER IS GIVING WORK TO A SCRUM TEAM MEMBER FROM OUTSIDE THE SPRINT?

When we talk about self-discipline in agile development, we are not just restricting our scope to the Scrum teams. If the *entire* organization does not embrace Scrum, there will be no end of dysfunctions that result. Scrum teams work best when they are allowed to focus and work in an uninterrupted style on their Sprint Goals. However, not even Scrum suggests that every team member must work full time on a Scrum team; therefore, the question is not what to do about managers assigning work to Scrum team members. The question that we need to address is, how much of the team member's time is to be devoted to the Scrum team and how much to outside pursuits?

Ideally, each team member on a Scrum team is 100% focused on the team goals, but the reality is that this cannot and, in fact, should not be attempted. Time should always be set aside for every employee to engage in some of the following:

- Personal career growth
- Technical skills improvement
- Process and practice improvement
- Community involvement and improvement

In addition to these items, team members will frequently be called on to provide

- Support in their area of expertise on other projects
- Coaching and development of less-experienced employees
- Other sundry and varied efforts

This, then, leaves us in a precarious balancing act between building the product, building the people, building the process, building the organization, and building the community. In the typical waterfall project, we generally set the "resource allocation" to 80% or 85% and base the task duration for the project on it.

In agile development, we essentially decide how much time we are willing to devote to other efforts and use the rest to get the Scrum team's work done. While this sounds a little backward, you have to remember that Scrum teams base their Sprint Goals on what they believe they can get done in the available time (which means, essentially, the time we have left). Frankly, this view of resource allocation is probably better as it forces the more difficult decisions to be made with regard to how to best employ our project resources. Once the "extra work" is decided, the team members can then commit to work during Sprint Planning to the extent that they are comfortable.

To make it easier, let us take an example.

A resource manager, Jeanne, has 10 developers who report to her and are on four different Scrum teams. Jeanne absolutely insists that her group works constantly on improving their skills and coaching others to improve. If possible, and if her employees are so inclined, she also allows some degree of participation in some of the community contact projects of the company. Each year, Jeanne's company goes through a budgeting process for the next fiscal year; they determine the priorities for the organization and how resources will be allocated to achieve those goals. Jeanne uses a "homegrown" worksheet to plan resource allocations. For 2010, it looked like Table 15.1, which shows a manager's attempt to budget her employee's time based on their experience. "Projects" time is how much each employee could commit to his or her Scrum team.

Jeanne gave everyone a 10% allocation for administrative tasks. For those employees with more than 2 years of experience, Jeanne allowed the choice to spend 5% of their time on community projects. The more experience the employee had, the less time spent on new skills and the more time spent on coaching (except for Faith, who had shown an interest in management, for which Jeanne agreed she was a good match). Each year she used a worksheet like this, Jeanne felt like it gave her and her group a good view of what to expect during the year—and each year was a little easier to plan than the previous year.

A few years ago, as Jeanne was just beginning to use the worksheet and as the transition to agile development was barely under way, Jeanne and

TABLE 15.1

Jeanne's Teams Time Budget

Name	Years Experience	Admin. (%)	Skills (%)	Coaching (%)	Community (%)	Projects (%)
Bill	2	10	20	0	0	70
Daphne	4	10	10	5	5	70
Jill	5	10	10	5	5	70
Vijay	2	10	20	0	0	70
Derek	4	10	10	5	5	70
Kavitha	2	10	20	0	0	70
Faith	7	10	15	5	5	65
Howard	9	10	5	15	5	65
Paul	8	10	5	15	5	65
Gail	9	10	5	15	5	65

her group were faced with all sorts of questions. For the most part, the conversation sounded something like this:

A quick knock on the door shook Jeanne out of her review of the recently completed resource allocation worksheet. "Come in," she called.

The door opened; it was Gail, Jeanne's most experienced developer. Gail was always among the first to see when something was wrong and would quickly raise the problem to discuss it and fix it. "Jeanne," Gail said, "I've reviewed the allocation worksheet, and I'm having a little problem."

Not at all surprised, Jeanne prompted, "Have a seat and tell me what you've found." Gail sat.

"I agree with the allocations in principle," Gail explained. "They make sense, and since we've all discussed them together, there are no surprises, but … "

"Go ahead," Jeanne said, leaning forward slightly in her chair, "I'm really curious now … "

"Well," Gail started, "I understand the numbers, but I don't see how we make them work."

Jeanne leaned back, not understanding the difficulty, but beginning to worry. "I don't quite understand. Could you explain?"

Her thoughts coming a little faster now, Gail continued confidently, "Well, when the project schedules are laid out, they take into account our project allocation as if every week was a precise echo of the allocation."

"Echo?" Jeanne, well, echoed.

"Yes," Gail said, barely stopping, "it's as if every week would be exactly 4 hours administrative, and 2 hours of skills work, and 6 hours of coaching, and so on. But it doesn't happen like that. Some weeks there's more coaching than others. Some weeks there's more administrative than others."

"Right," Jeanne said, starting to understand the direction, "but it all equals out in the end, doesn't it?"

"Somewhat," Gail conceded, "but it tends to work against us. If we happen to have a few weeks when we get more project tasks done, the project manager increases our project allocation to make the plan more accurate. But if we then have weeks when we aren't as productive on the project tasks as the good weeks, we're falling behind. When we fall behind, we're expected to use the other allocations to make up for the delays. Before we're 3 months into the year, the allocations are all gone—all we have is a little administrative time and a huge project allocation."

"I see," Jeanne said, beginning to consider the problem in her head. Jeanne came from a programming background as well, so the scenario described by Gail did not seem out of line at all. Playing the role of a good coach (and recognizing she did not have a good answer yet), Jeanne asked, "What would you suggest?"

"Honestly," Gail admitted, "I'm not sure yet."

As the organization began to adopt agile development, however, the answer slowly became more evident. Gail had diagnosed the problem without actually realizing it; while the average of the more productive weeks and the less-productive weeks would have worked out in the long run, the reality is that the organization quickly lost sight of the long-term allocations in the face of short-term schedule slippages. What Scrum does, however, is create a sort of "reset" condition at the end of each Sprint.

In our story of Jeanne and her group, what they discovered was that they would consider their planned allocations at the beginning of every 4-week Sprint. For example, Howard would go into the Sprint Planning knowing that he would plan to use 4 hours a week (10%) for administrative work, 1 day (5% = 2 hours × 4 weeks) during the Sprint for skills improvement, 6 hours a week (15%) for coaching, and 1 day (5%) during the Sprint for community projects. He did not know exactly when all of this would occur, but he knew that he needed to be careful how much he committed to do during the Sprint so that he did not cause the team to overcommit.

At first, everyone on the team was a little concerned that he or she would be unable to "feel out" or "guess" at the right level of commitment. Team members were concerned that they might overcommit or undercommit. In the end, however, the proper level of commitment was determined by the team during the first few Sprints, and any necessary corrections to the team's commitment were made during the Sprint without any loss of productivity.

So, team members on a Scrum team having work to do other than the work on the team's Sprint Backlog are not uncommon. However, having explained how this is supposed to work, let us take a few minutes to discuss the abuse of a team member's allocation.

In some cases, when planned allocations give way to managers assigning additional work to Scrum team members, there are several steps that should be taken. First, it is important to assume that the manager is unaware of the "rules" of the Scrum framework and is therefore unaware of the effect that his or her "assignments" are having on the Scrum team. Someone will need to fully explain the situation to the manager in question; exactly who will do so depends heavily on the attitude and character of the manager. Perhaps the team member himself or herself can explain the situation. On the other hand, it may take another manager more highly placed in the organizational structure.

Second, it is worthwhile to dig a little deeper and find out how well educated management is in general with regard to agile development. I have seen many implementations of agile development for which the training of management was forgotten once the training of the executives, the teams, and the Product Owners was completed.

While this situation is continuing, the team member who is getting additional assignments from his or her manager has two choices: (a) continue to make the team's commitment a priority and do the additional work as time permits or (b) do the additional work as a priority and help achieve the team's commitment as time permits. In the former case, the dysfunction caused by the extra assignments will cause friction between the employee and the manager and will likely be addressed as a result of unmet expectations. In the latter case, the team's loss of velocity will call attention to the team's performance, bringing to light the dysfunction caused by the extra assignments. One way or another, the problem of the extra assignments will be raised. The ultimate and final question is simply, how will the organization solve the obvious dysfunction?

MY DAILY SCRUM HAS TURNED INTO A 1-HOUR STATUS MEETING! WHY?

It is actually fairly easy for a Daily Scrum, which should be only 15 minutes for a proper size Scrum team, to turn into 30 minutes, 45 minutes, or even (in the worst case I have seen) 1 hour. Doing a Daily Scrum properly takes an appreciation for the purpose of the Daily Scrum and the ability to exercise and enforce the discipline of how the Daily Scrum works.

The Daily Scrum is an integral part of the "inspect-and-adapt" framework of Scrum. When done properly, it provides an opportunity for the team to *inspect* what is going on around them (Did the nightly build fail? Is someone out sick today? Did we finish the backlog item we were planning to finish yesterday? Are there any other teams around us in trouble?). That is, in fact, why team members answer the questions: What have I done since the last meeting? and What do I plan to do before the next meeting? These questions form the basis for inspection and when answered with enough detail to be informative, but briefly enough that a team member answers the questions in a little less than 2 minutes, the questions *are* the inspection.

Unfortunately, many of us have been taught to answer questions in extensive detail. Some of us have not learned how to provide a simple and unembellished report of our status. Honestly, some of us just like to hear ourselves talk (I guess the more we say, the better we sound). When our tendencies to speak at length are not curbed properly, the length of the Daily Scrum increases. This is where the ScrumMaster comes in.

A good ScrumMaster will participate in the Daily Scrum, carefully watching how long the Daily Scrum is taking and considering how effective the Daily Scrum actually is. Daily Scrums should not regularly take longer than 15 minutes. When they do, it is up to the ScrumMaster to begin shortening team member responses by asking everyone to stick to the basics: What task did you work on? What problems are you having? When do you plan to be finished? Also, it is usually normal for team members to ask clarifying questions during the Daily Scrum. Sometimes, however, the questions begin a longer conversation that the ScrumMaster should encourage be deferred until after everyone has had an opportunity. While many people feel uncomfortable telling others to wait, remember that you are really only asking that person to wait for something less than 15 minutes. That is not that much of a delay.

In addition, the ScrumMaster has to be careful with regard to questions or comments coming from those who may be attending the Daily Scrum but are not on the Scrum team. These people, by definition, are *not* permitted to speak during the Daily Scrum—whether they are an employee, a manager, or the president of the company, the ScrumMaster must ask the speaker to wait until the Daily Scrum is over.

Now, why is it so important to answer the three questions during the Sprint without interruption or delay? The reason has to do with the Daily Scrum being *the* mechanism by which inspect and adapt works on a daily basis during the Sprint. When the entire Scrum team gets together to answer these questions, they create a "picture" of their "current reality." The more they understand about the current reality, the more effective are the decisions that can be made when the team adapts. If their understanding is interrupted by other questions or their understanding is crippled by overly detailed and lengthy responses, the decisions that the team makes are less effective. Less-effective decisions can lead to failed Sprints.

WHAT DOES IT LOOK LIKE WHEN A SCRUM TEAM IS FAILING?

The variety of failure modes for Scrum teams is a litany that will likely continue to grow over the next several years as we get increasing experience with Scrum teams in many different environments. I attempt in this section to define as many as I possibly can and provide likely causes. However, I stop short of providing solutions in this section because either I may have already done so elsewhere in this book or there are far too many possible solutions to even begin to provide a worthwhile guide.

Failure Mode 1: Team Does Not Understand Scrum

I chose an obvious failure mode to begin. In this situation, the team may or may not have received proper training on what Scrum is and how it is used, but the training has not been effective or the team members were unable to internalize or use the training to their advantage. In either case, this failure mode is exhibited by improperly run Sprint Planning meetings, Daily Scrum meetings, Sprint Review meetings, and Sprint Retrospective meetings. The fundamental goals of the meetings are not understood, and the team essentially exhibits waterfall mannerisms couched in Scrum terms. You will frequently hear, "Well, that's what the book says!"

Failure Mode 2: Scummerfall

In the scummerfall mode of failure, the team has learned some of the form of Scrum but has misunderstood the concepts and probably lacks effective coaching. In scrummerfall sprints, a waterfall-like workflow is observed, with analysis and design work occurring at the beginning of the sprint, coding in the middle of the sprint, and testing and validation occurring at the end of the sprint, and frequently not finished by the end of the sprint. The team will suffer the same quality problems that plague waterfall projects, but they will do so iteratively. This failure mode is exhibited by a series of tasks like "analyze registration pathway," "design registration pathway," "build registration pathway," and "test registration pathway" (a waterfall approach has been applied to Sprint Backlog tasks). In a more extreme, although less-common variation, the team plans to do all of the analysis during the first couple days of the Sprint, all of their design during the next couple days, all of their coding next, and then all of their testing. The number of days allocated to each phase depends on the length of the Sprint; for example, in a 4-week Sprint you would have an analysis week, a design week, a coding week, and a testing week. On digging further, you might even discover evidence of a misapplication of the V model (see "Can I Use the V Model in My Sprints?" in Chapter 13).

Failure Mode 3: Command and Control

In this failure mode, either the ScrumMaster or a manager takes authority for the team's actions and decisions. This is frequently caused by (a) a misunderstanding of the concepts of self-management and self-organization, (b) deliberate action undertaken because the organization or the individual does not believe that the team can or should self-manage, or (c) nondeliberate action by someone who thinks he or she is helping the team when really the person is sapping the team's need to self-manage and self-organize. This mode of failure is exhibited by ScrumMasters or managers making decisions, rather than coaching the team to make most decisions on their own. You may also see ScrumMasters assigning tasks to team members.

Failure Mode 4: External Task Assignment

In this failure mode, managers are assigning their employees on Scrum teams additional work, above and beyond the commitment made by the Scrum team to the Product Owner. Often, the employee does not know how to respond to this situation, deciding finally to work on team tasks and on the extra assignments. With luck, and some overtime, the employee is sometimes successful. However, it usually does not take long before the extra work being done by the employee comes to the attention of the Scrum team and becomes a problem for the team *and* the employee as work takes longer to be completed and the stress level on the team rises precipitously. Eventually, the employee's extra work results in one or more backlog items being delayed such that an item cannot be finished by the end of the Sprint. As a result of the visibility offered by Scrum, it does not take the team long to figure out what happened to the delayed and unfinished backlog item. The problems get worse from there. This mode of failure usually begins to surface during the Daily Scrum when one or more employees indicate that they are still working on the same task as the day before due to other work assigned by their manager. It often reaches its peak during Sprint Retrospective meetings, when the employee is confronted with regard to the delays and encouraged to follow up with his or her manager to stop assigning the extra work.

If the employee is successful in stopping the extra work, the team often survives this failure mode. However, should the extra assignments continue, there are a couple possible paths along which the failure may accelerate. First, the team might begin to limit the types of tasks and the extent of the commitment that the suffering employee may volunteer to do. This often leads to significant internal strife, pushing the team into a "storming" state from which there may be no way to escape. Second, the team might ostracize the employee entirely, which may also result in a storming state or, at least, a significantly reduced velocity and lower morale (quite possibly, both the storming and the lower velocity will occur).

Failure Mode 5: Backlog Items Are Too Big

In this failure mode, the team goes to Sprint Planning with backlog items that each take up a significant percentage of the size of the Sprint. As a result, Sprint Planning is either difficult or impossible to finish in a single day and sometimes continues to a second or even a third day before a Sprint Backlog and a commitment can be derived. Larger backlog items tend to regularly spawn previously unknown requirements or other risks, causing the team to add more tasks to their Sprint Backlog, which eventually leads to significant overcommitment. By the end of the Sprint, the team is unable to actually complete any backlog items and carries the remaining work into the next Sprint, further exacerbating the backlog size problem by reducing the overall amount of time in the Sprint for new work because of the need to complete the work of the previous Sprint. This leads to unpredictability and, more important, frustration and discontent on the team.

This failure mode is characterized by (a) incomplete or nonconstructive Sprint Planning meetings, (b) pressure by the team to do "preplanning" a few days before the end of the previous Sprint, (c) lack of backlog grooming during the previous Sprint, and (d) significant upward spikes sometimes accompanied by lengthy horizontal periods in the Sprint Burndown.

Failure Mode 6: Poor Team Self-Management

In the failure mode related to poor team self-management, every time the team finishes a Sprint, it is discovered that some aspect of DONEness or other operational procedure for which they are responsible is not getting done. This results in a lot of frustration with the team and frustration with the Scrum framework itself. The organization often presses for more management oversight of the Scrum team, which unfortunately results in the further erosion of Scrum and agile development.

This mode of failure is exhibited by extreme frustration outside the team; the team, on the other hand, usually does not realize that anything is wrong, or if they do realize that things are not getting done, the team is quick to point out that someone else is responsible. This is, more often than not, a problem with the team's self-managing abilities. Self-managing teams are responsible for understanding everything they are expected to do in the normal course of building production software. When they clearly forgot or were not aware, the self-managing teams take steps to ensure that a mistake made once is not repeated. They take responsibility for what they produce and take steps, without being asked or reminded, to ensure that any mistake can occur only once.

Failure Mode 7: Anti-Self-Management

In the anti-self-management failure mode, the Scrum team has decided that being an agile development team excuses them from (a) using good development practices or (b) following organizational policies. This mode of failure usually can be diagnosed by listening to the team's reactions to either being asked to do something they do not feel they should have to do or being told they are not actually done with a backlog item that they said they had finished. The team's typical reaction to either is to say that, "We don't do that, we're agile," and "That's not our job; that's the Product Owner's problem."

This mode of failure is a variation on the self-management team. Someone has sold agile to the team by focusing on all the stuff that the team will not have to do anymore and how it empowers the team to make their own decisions without relating the fact that being empowered and making decisions requires the team also to be accountable for what they do and how they do it. Some teams deliberately turn a deaf ear to self-management; others simply do not know what it means when they hear it. In all cases, significant remedial training and coaching are needed to reset everyone's expectations.

Failure Mode 8: Team Is Too Big

In Scrum, teams are preferred to be no smaller than five team members and no larger than nine. While this is not an unbreakable rule, I have found many more dysfunctions on teams of 10, 12, and 15. The reason for this guideline is the practical reality of inspection and adaptation. For a team to be able to effectively inspect and adapt on a regular basis, they need a small enough working environment that they can easily understand what is going on around them and can then make practical and effective adaptation decisions about what they know.

Imagine being in a Daily Scrum with a team of 15. Everyone, yourself included, answers the three typical questions of the Daily Scrum (What did you do since the previous meeting? What do you plan to do between now and the next meeting? What, if anything, is getting in the way of getting tasks done?). Now, try to remember what the first person who answered those questions said. Can you? If you can, try to relate what that person said to the answers provided by the other team members. Can you? Does anything you heard raise any concern?

This is the danger of creating a team that is too big. They cannot adapt. Daily Scrum meetings end with everyone having a vague feeling of dissatisfaction. Good decisions cannot be made, and it often falls on one or two people to make the decisions or for the team to simply become more reactive, responding to events rather than planning for them. As a result, the opportunity to achieve increasingly higher velocities is often lost, with the team showing, perhaps, modest gains, but nothing like they might achieve in a smaller and more easily adapted setting.

In this failure mode, teams generally wither. They may stay together (depending on the expectations of the organization), but they rarely become high-performing teams, achieving high velocities and excellent self-management.

Failure Mode 9: ScrumMaster Does Not Provide Leadership

While it is true that the ScrumMaster is not a manager and exercises no authority over the team, the typical Scrum team nonetheless enjoys having a ScrumMaster who can exhibit a certain amount of leadership on a regular basis. The Scrum team wants to know that there is someone watching out for their interests, protecting the team, working with the Product Owner and resolving problems, and keeping the team focused in discussions and arguments.

When the ScrumMaster does not or cannot provide both the leadership and the sense of protection, the team tends to become frustrated. In a variation on this problem, someone else on the team steps up to handle what the ScrumMaster is not handling. While this tends to help the team in one way, it does nothing to alleviate the frustration that the team is feeling.

Observable symptoms of this problem are a lack of energy and enthusiasm on the part of the team, a potential falloff in collaborative behaviors and velocity, and a ScrumMaster who is usually at his or her desk, updating documents, updating the backlog management tool, creating reports, or attending meetings unrelated to the Scrum team's activities.

REFERENCE

Covey, Stephen R. 2004. *The 8th Habit: From Effectiveness to Greatness*. New York, NY: Simon & Schuster.

Schiel, James A. 2010. *Enterprise-Scale Agile Software Development*. Boca Raton, FL: CRC Press.

Schwaber, Ken and Beedle, Mike. 2002. *Agile Software Development with Scrum*. Saddle River, NJ: Prentice Hall.

Index